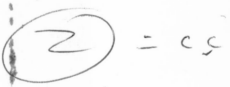

The Horseman's Bedside Book

THE HORSEMAN'S
BEDSIDE BOOK

Edited by
Lieutenant-Colonel J. A. Talbot-Ponsonby

London
B. T. BATSFORD LTD

First published 1964

Made and printed in Great Britain by
William Clowes and Sons Ltd, London and Beccles
for the publishers B. T. BATSFORD LTD
4 Fitzhardinge Street, Portman Square, London W.1

CONTENTS

Contents

EDITOR'S NOTE

ENJOYMENT DERIVED from reading a book with a title such as this one bears can be agreeably arguable. I suppose that it must depend upon the state of mind the reader wishes to obtain before slumber takes command. Does he wish to have his senses captivated by a thrilling story, in which case he may well read on throughout the night? Does he hope that wit and humour will dissipate his everyday worries, and so induce sleep with a smile? Would he rather browse on technical theories, giving his brain work to do without rest? Or, through sheer boredom, will he prefer to relapse rapidly into deep-throated snoring, with the light still on, and the book open on his chest? A ticklish problem indeed, but one that can only be resolved by the patient himself.

This book attempts to cater for some at least of these tastes. The authors who have kindly contributed towards it are not all, by any means, in the habit of putting pen to paper for any other than private reasons. Although all are intensely interested in the horse, and some in specialised riding also, there are a few among them whose names are more often linked with industrial affairs, who have spent valuable time in making their first journey into the literary world. Some of the stories give true pictures of very famous occasions, some are based on fact, but all show clearly the very close relationship that has always existed between the horse and the inhabitants of these islands. Although many people have never ridden, either from personal choice, or by virtue of the pattern of their lives, there are few who do not admire the horse as an elegant and attractive animal, with a very special niche in the realm of sport.

For centuries the horse has been part and parcel of English life. Always a willing servant, and ever a faithful friend, he has afforded pleasure to millions, even if it be only to the extent of having two bob on the 3.30! So, as a prelude to a period of beautiful sleep, rather than count numberless some-

7

Editor's Note

what dreary sheep through a hedge, let us consider the horse in his various roles, and a rider's hopes and problems. To those of us who have spent their lives with horses, the loss of a favourite is a very cruel blow indeed. I like to hope that the horse's prayer may always be answered:

> *To Thee oh my master I offer my prayer.*
>
> *My life and health I give to your safe keeping;*
> *From you I ask food and water,*
> *Shelter in winter and summer,*
> *A kind hand and a quiet voice.*
> *And when I am old*
> *And have served you well;*
> *Pray, Oh, my Master,*
> *Do not sell me to slavery and to a cruel end.*

Autumn, 1964   J.A. T-P.

ACKNOWLEDGMENT

THE EDITOR AND THE PUBLISHERS are greatly indebted to the following for supplying the photographs which appear on the pages given after their names, and for their permission to reproduce them in this book:

Mr. Eric Ager, page 76; Austrian State Tourist Department, page 168; Bertram Mills Circus Ltd., page 139; Black Star Publishing Co. Ltd., pages 106, 107, 216; Mr. Rex Coleman, pages 35, 61, 75, 126, 221; Keystone Press Agency Ltd., pages 20, 30, 36, 125; Mr. Frank H. Meads, pages 13 top, 14, 19, 55 top, 56, 69, 70, 100, 189; Mr. Nicholas Meyjes and the Editor of *The Field*, pages 55 bottom, 62, 99, 152 top, 157, 190 bottom; Miles Brothers, page 152 bottom; "Monty", page 195; Mr. John Nestle, pages 211, 212, 215; Paul Popper Ltd., pages 29, 89, 105 bottom, 218; Reed Photography, pages 90, 167; Sport & General Agency Ltd., pages 13 bottom, 105 top, 108, 145, 146, 190 top, 217, 222; Thomson Newspapers Ltd., page 151.

They also acknowledge with thanks the permission of William Collins Sons & Co. Ltd. to include the essay "Behind the Scenes" from *Youth in the Saddle*, and that of the Editor of *Horse and Hound* for his permission to reproduce the article "A Winter's Tale" from the issue of 23 June, 1962. "Hounds" by Captain R. E. Wallace is reprinted from *Country Life* (26 September, 1963) by permission of the Editor.

The text decorations and the dust jacket were designed by Miss Joan Wanklyn.

From Point-to-Point

MICHAEL WILLIAMS

ANYONE WOULD THINK, to hear some people talk, that the modern point-to-point is an invention of the Devil, and that all that is lacking to make it 100 per cent diabolical is the celebration of the Black Mass before racing.

The variations on this theme have rung in the ear of successive generations, and will no doubt be served up with relish to future ones. I first heard them twenty years ago, from a much respected hunting correspondent, who maintained that the point-to-point had "become a species of bastard race-meeting", and complained indignantly that it was "run for profit and with prizes competed for by horses principally kept for the purpose, and barely qualified as hunters (even under the very lax rules imposed for such quali-fication) . . .".

That hunting correspondent has now reached a venerable age and is, I am happy to say, still going strong, both in the saddle and out of it. But many years before he was born (I imagine), similar sentiments were being expressed by Surtees in *Mr. Sponge's Sporting Tour*. To Surtees, point-to-points were "crude ill-arranged things—neither hunting nor racing". Even in 1853, apparently, the "regularly and fairly hunted" brigade, accord-ing to Surtees, were engaged in "a regularity than which nothing could be more irregular".

Time changes everything, except the die-hards. Today there is a whole new public for point-to-point racing, and it is a highly demanding one, no longer content with the spectacle of a handful of heavy-weights disappearing into the distance at half-speed. It likes a race to be a race, and it couldn't care less how much or how little the horses have been hunted beforehand. And since the primary aim of a point-to-point is to make some money for the hunt, it follows that the organisers are concerned to make the sport as attractive as possible to participants and spectators alike.

The least that is necessary to win an open point-to-point nowadays is a blood horse with some pretensions to racing ability, piloted by a rider who isn't ashamed to look like a steeplechase jockey. Most of all, however, the courses have changed. Those bedraggled-looking "natural" fences surrounded by acres of ploughland are things of the past. Vast sums of money are expended on the upkeep of today's point-to-point courses, and there is keen competition to secure the best sites and the best fence-builders. A fine point-to-point course is regarded with justifiable pride, and it is significant that when it comes to advertising there is often more emphasis put on the course than on the hunt that is promoting the meeting. In many instances, the same course serves several hunts. In 1964 Larkhill and Tweseldown led with five fixtures apiece, and all the indications are that the process of centralisation is steadily gathering momentum.

Of course, those of us who can remember the old-style point-to-point course are apt to look back on it with nostalgia, though this doesn't necessarily mean that we wish to see it revived. At my local point-to-point before the war (the second one), we watched the horses jump the first two fences, ran like stags to see their behinds vanishing over the next two, and waited in suspense for them to reappear over the last two. What went on in the country, out of sight of the Stewards, was anybody's guess, and sometimes the guessing was extremely libellous, particularly on the occasions when a totally unexpected leader appeared on the horizon.

Those were the days when Ryan Price (now one of our leading trainers) was riding in point-to-points, and a very devil-may-care figure he cut as he rode out of the paddock smoking a cigarette—a sight that as often as not so filled his admirers with confidence that they felt obliged to approach the bookmakers with a further request for the mixture as before. I suppose he was worth about 2 stone over most of his local rivals. In those days the rider was all-important; and as the wrong names were frequently being put up on the board, it was sometimes possible to catch the bookmaking fraternity napping. Now, although it still pays to consider the riders, it is usually necessary to take the horses into account as well.

I think it was probably before my time when a bystander could remount a riderless horse, ride a stirring finish on it, and expect to keep the race if he won. And I cannot claim to have been present when a bunch of "the boys", seeing that all was lost, overturned the judge's wagon and kept that worthy gentleman pinned underneath it until the winner had passed the post, thus ensuring that the race would be declared void.

An old-fashioned look, but still great sport for everyone

Turning for home at Tweseldown, Aldershot—an adjacent Hunt's Ladies race

For the ladies' fashions change, and styles differ

"I would like to know just how the hell you think I could have remained in the saddle when my horse went arse over tip"

From Point-to-Point

But I can certainly give the lie to the people who say that all the colour has gone out of point-to-point racing. Within the last few years I have seen two well-known lady riders doing their best to ride each other down. I have seen two gentlemen riders using their whips on each other in the course of a race. I have been present at a fracas in the men's dressing-tent, and heard tell of language used in the ladies' dressing-tent that would put the fruit porters in Covent Garden to shame. I have even heard one point-to-point tipster calling another a ponce. And, not so long ago in the Cotswolds, I recall the following exchange between a popular turf adviser and a member of his audience:

"How dare you say those things about my husband!"

"I'm very sorry madam, but I can only speak as I find; and I find that your husband couldn't ride in a bus without falling out of it," a statement with which, after the race, I found myself much in sympathy.

So long as the university point-to-points continue to prosper, there is not likely to be any shortage of amusing incidents, and the Oxford University Bullingdon Club have provided quite a few in their time. I have vivid memories of one such incident, because I was among the fortunate punters who profited from the result, though not one of those who assisted in obtaining it. The maiden race that day was an astonishing affair. At one stage all four riders were on the floor. And when, eventually, one of the partnerships was successfully renewed, and actually managed to reach the last fence, horse and rider once more parted company. It looked like being a "skinner" for the books, until a group of enthusiastic spectators developed other ideas, seized hold of the horse fore and aft and hustled him over the fence, leaving the rider to make his own way over and rejoin his mount in the run-in. To the delight of their supporters, and the indignation of the bookmakers, who knew more about the rules than the Stewards, the pair were then declared the winners.

The university meetings do not exactly have a prerogative of such incidents, however. I recall a similar case of unauthorised assistance at a meeting in Kent. On this occasion the remaining survivor of a small field showed so much reluctance as he approached the final obstacle that there was a distinct danger of his stopping altogether. The suspense proved too much for one sportsman, who quickly ducked under the ropes and gave the animal a resounding blow across the buttocks with his field glasses. It was said afterwards that the horse jumped the fence out of sheer surprise.

Sometimes, of course, things work the other way, and I would not advise any point-to-point rider to do what Steve Donoghue used to do, and specialise in winning by short heads. And sometimes half a length is not enough, for the Judges at some meetings appear to belong to a school that has very old-fashioned ideas, to put it no more strongly than that. I was once given a lift off the course by one of these gentlemen, who, mellowed by several glasses of port—or perhaps it was cherry brandy—solemnly addressed me as follows: "What I always say is that if two horses run a genuine race and finish within three lengths of each other over three miles, then they deserve to be given a dead-heat, what?"

The older one gets, the more one learns; and those of us who write about point-to-point racing are always learning, usually the hard way. And one of the things I have learned is that there is nothing a third-class rider dislikes more than reading that he has ridden a second-class race. Fortunately, amateurs rarely go to the lengths of some of the professionals and threaten libel actions. The editor of a well-known sporting paper once told me with glee that he could paper the walls of his office with letters from jockeys threatening to sue him. "Although," he added wistfully, "whereas in the past it was always the jockeys themselves who wrote in, now it is usually their solicitors."

Naturally, no rider takes kindly to the suggestion that he has ridden a bad race, particularly if it is justified; and for most amateur riders the word "unseated" is a very dirty word indeed. I am careful, nowadays, not to use such a word unless I can justify it up to the hilt. It is much safer to use some euphemistic phrase as "came to grief", since it is difficult for the reader to deduce the exact meaning of it. Besides, it reduces the chances of having to answer letters which begin, like the one I got from an Officers' Mess: "I would like to know just how the hell you think I could have remained in the saddle when my horse went arse over tip!"

But if one is kind to the rider, then as likely as not one will hear from the owner. To write that a horse fell when, technically, he may not have done is even more dangerous than saying that a rider was unseated when, technically, he may not have been. I have had more letters from owners than from riders, and few unsolicited ones have been complimentary. If one writes something nice about a horse, it is taken for granted. But if one writes something uncomplimentary, such as, for instance, "I am afraid he is no longer in love with the game", it nearly always turns out that the owner has been trying to sell the horse and considers that his prospects of doing so have been damaged.

For some owners a rider can do nothing right. If he wins, it is the horse who gets all the credit for it. And if he loses, and dares to suggest that the horse would not run his race properly, or that the winner was better, he is likely to find himself looking elsewhere for rides. "You were much too kind to my rider," a lady wrote to me last season. "The truth is, he ought

From Point-to-Point

to be horse whipped." It is a pity, perhaps, that the lady couldn't have heard what her ex-rider had to say about her when I saw him on the course shortly afterwards.

Owner-riders are naturally in a specially privileged position. They can hardly be expected to give themselves the sack, although I have sometimes been tempted to suggest it, never more so than on a certain occasion last season. Against the advice of a knowledgeable friend, who assured me that not even Mill House would win a race with this rider on top, I decided to help myself over what I considered to be the good thing of the day. I reasoned that the animal in question had at least a stone in hand and that, barring an Act of God, he couldn't possibly lose, since he was also a notably safe conveyance. And when the "good thing" came to the last fence with the proverbial ton in hand, four lengths ahead of his nearest rival, a notorious plodder, I was already congratulating myself. But a lot can happen between the last fence and the winning post, and on this occasion it did. The rider of the plodder, evidently well aware of his opponent's shortcomings in the art of riding a finish, got down to work with a vengeance, and of course won the race.

To make matters worse, as the rider of the runner-up was returning to the paddock I heard someone commiserating with him on his hard luck. It wasn't his groom. That gentleman was moving shakily in the direction of the bar, where what he had to say about his Lord and Master was nobody's business. But it seemed to boil down to the fact that his present employment was costing him a fortune.

When I was asked to write this article I warned the Editor, before accepting the assignment, that my idea of an article for a Bedside Book might not coincide with his and that, with whatever good intentions I might start out, I should probably end up writing the sort of thing that I liked to read in bed myself.

"But that's just what I want," he said. "Your function will be to give our readers a breather. At the same time," he added, meaningly, "I shall expect you to incorporate some useful tips on the art of point-to-point riding."

I have given some thought to the matter, and it has not taken me long to arrive at the conclusion that the best I can do is to pick the brains of the most successful of all living point-to-point riders. So here, for the enlightenment of readers who have got this far, is a list of Do's and Don'ts that has been very kindly given to me by Major Guy Cunard:

DON'T walk the course in the opposite direction conversing as you go.

DO walk the course just as you would ride it—alone if you can.

DON'T eat a good lunch or have a drink before you ride.

DO ride on as near an empty stomach as you comfortably can.

From Point-to-Point

DON'T have a hard-and-fast plan of campaign.

DO have a flexible plan that can be amended if things do not go as anticipated. Remember, your horse won't always run as expected.

DON'T decide that you are a certainty, or that you have no chance, because of what the self-appointed experts who juggle with handicap ratings have had to say about your horse.

DO ride every race with an open mind. All those ratings that have been compiled on past form will be knocked for six as soon as the new season starts.

DON'T allow yourself to be caught unawares at the start.

DO be alert and ready to get a good start.

DON'T decide the sort of race to ride without considering what suits your horse.

DO ride the sort of race which suits your horse's peculiarities and way of running. In a nutshell, adapt yourself to your horse and do not expect him to adapt himself to you.

DON'T decide to sit right up your horse's neck over a jump in order to be caught looking pretty by the camera; or decide to sit right back either, as there is a drop to a fence.

DO keep BALANCED over your fences.

DON'T keep a tight hold of your horse's head at his fences.

DO give your horse a free head, and plenty of rein to land with. If necessary, let the reins slip through your fingers and prop them up afterwards.

DON'T try to pass another competitor by attempting to squeeze between him and a flag.

DO go round him or, better still, sit in behind him and pass him on the straight.

DON'T go flat out uphill.

DO, if you can, give your horse an easy when going uphill.

DON'T get boxed in in a crowd, or jump immediately on another horse's tail.

DO try to give your horse a good view of his fences.

DON'T ease your horse up going into the last fence.

DO see that your horse is properly balanced before taking the last fence, and then kick him hard into it.

DON'T stop riding before the winning post, or even ease up.

DO ride as hard as you can until you are safely PAST the winning post.

DON'T drop your reins or pick up your whip to ride a finish.

DO hold your horse together, and ride him out with your legs.

DON'T ride a tired horse right out when he has no chance of being placed.

DO ride a tired horse quietly and, if necessary, pull him up.

I hope things may not be quite as bad as they seem!

DON'T, if you are lucky enough to ride a winner, take all the credit.

DO give most of the credit to the horse. He has done all the work.

To these wise maxims all I have to add is this. SIT STILL in the saddle, and, unless you want to make sure of ending up in hospital, LIE STILL after a fall until the rest of the field has passed by. And, for pity's sake, don't look over your shoulder approaching a fence or between the last fence and the winning post.

Finally, a quotation from a great amateur of another day, John Hislop:

> *. . . the most important properties in the*
> *embryo steeplechase-rider are, an unquenchable*
> *enthusiasm, and a real love and appreciation*
> *of the horse—in particular, the racehorse.*

The first Grand National was run on 26 February, 1839, being called the Grand Liverpool steeplechase. A sweepstake of 20 sovs. each 5 sovs. forfeit, with 100 sovs. added. It must be remembered that the course lay over a natural country, deep plough, ridge and furrow, low ground where the rain lay, cart-rutted tracks, and muddy gateways.

I will say that I would look forward with the greatest pleasure to another ride at Aintree, but shudder at the thought of riding in the Maryland Hunt Cup again.

NOEL LAING

. . . there have been great jumping jockeys who were not at a disadvantage with a flat-race jockey in a finish. The greatest jockey on the flat, over hurdles, or the stiffest steeplechase course during my time was Fred Rees.

STEVE DONOGHUE

may be a bit of a lad, but I do love my freedom

Riding for the Million

LIEUT.-COLONEL C. E. G. HOPE

A POPULAR PASTIME amongst "oldies" is looking back on the "good old days". Ex-cavalry officers in their cups are particularly prone to it—old "squares" that we are. Through misty eyes or the bottoms of glasses we look back to a sort of paradise for horsemen—and horses—in an age when there were no motor cars—or hardly any, when income tax was a shilling in the pound and you could get a bottle of whisky for four shillings—the hey-day of the horse. But was it really?

I know that the horse population has declined catastrophically since those days. It ran into millions at the turn of the century; by 1954 it was 300,000; now I should think the tally would not run out above 75,000. Yet, looking back fifty-odd years, I am quite sure that I see while out and about on my lawful occasions many more people on horseback then I ever did in the country before World War I, which still remains the watershed between two epochs. More horses, yes, I grant you that, but certainly not more *riders*.

The horses and ponies one saw most of were in harness, professional working horses for the most part, whom the automobile had not yet supplanted. I know that one saw a lot of riders at hunt meets or playing polo in the select social enclaves of Hurlingham, Ranelagh and Roehampton, or of a Sunday morning in the Row; and of course in military stations. Even they, however, were in a minority; if the Olympia catalogue of 1907—the first International Horse Show—is any guide. Then, out of 124 classes no less than 85 were for harness horses and ponies of some category or other; there were 11 jumping classes; the remaining 28 classes included hacks, hunters, polo ponies and riding ponies. There is nostalgic reading for you! By 1935 the situation had changed. Out of 90 classes at Olympia, harness claimed 35, jumping 9; the remaining 46 riding classes including a dressage class in which was a horse called Ecstasy ridden by Captain J. E. Hance, who died in January 1964.

In 1963 the catalogue of the Royal International Horse Show, at White City, listed 57 classes. Of these jumping took up 19, riding classes 19, the harness classes 19. These, it is interesting to note, included a private driving marathon and 3 private driving competitions, the whirligig of time thus bringing a small revenge. The growth of keenness for driving as a sport is a marked feature of the equestrian history of the 'sixties. Among the riding classes in the 1963 White City schedule was one that has appeared there since 1957—the Riding Clubs Teams Competition. This it is that really epitomises the change that has come over the riding scene from the so-called good old days of 50 and 60 years ago until the present time.

It is the difference between riding for the few and riding for the million. In the past, as I have suggested, the horse was essentially a workman. He still is a worker, of course, but his work is different and the people he works for are different. Of course this is a generalisation, but it is broadly true. The horse-drawn vehicle has virtually disappeared from the roads, except when the valiant members of the British Driving Society and the Coaching Club proceed on their marathons and meets. The Army has on its establishment about 500 horses, mostly for ceremonial purposes. The closely-knit polo world still has its little social enclave, now at Cowdray and Windsor. The hunting world remains more or less where it was; there are actually more hunts in existence in 1964 than there were sixty years ago. To be precise, according to Baily's there are 28 more packs now than there were in 1903. On the other hand the fields are not so large, certainly not larger than the enormous crowds that used to collect in the Shires during the 'thirties.

Yet, in the country and on the outskirts of towns there are more actual riders to be seen, especially on a Saturday, than ever there were in the past: strings of riders from riding schools, children coming and going from Pony Club rallies, riding club members having instructional rides in somebody's field, and horse shows. There are over a thousand horse shows affiliated to the British Show Jumping Association, and many more unofficial gymkhanas, hunter trials and Riding Clubs and Pony Club events of all kinds. The whole country teems with equestrian activity more than ever before. Incidentally I have not included the police and the thoroughbred world in these comparisons, because whatever madness overcomes our society these two institutions seem to be the most stable of all. We manifestly cannot do without the police—or anyway their horses—and life would be really unthinkable somehow without the thoroughbred. But these other changes are definite and unmistakable; they are part of a wider social revolution which is still going on.

The point is that fifty years ago only the high and mighty rode, the people whose houses, according to Bernard Shaw, were only annexes to the stables; now everybody rides.

It happened in the early 'thirties. Nobody knows how or why, but the office workers, especially girls, discovered the horse. Perhaps it was a result of the general emancipation that took place during World War I, when all our lives were turned upside down for good and all, for better or worse—it depends on how one was placed before that war. However that may be, such riding establishments as existed began to be patronised by a new kind of clientèle—the week-end rider.

The high and mighty still remained, of course, and Olympia became their annual re-union; but as the Army became mechanised their numbers decreased, though not, fortunately, their influence. They became a numerical minority in the horse world, but they kept alive the best features of the old days, the elegance, the traditions, and the expertise—the knowledge and practice of the art of horsemanship. So the two parties married, as it were, and produced the equestrian set-up of today. But for it all and for the survival of the horse into the atomic age we have to thank the week-end rider.

In the days between the wars I think that the old and new riding worlds were fairly represented by the two societies—the Institute of the Horse and the National Horse Association. After the war the former body was hard put to it to survive; it was saved by the amalgamation with the then stronger body, the N.H.A. The result was the British Horse Society, which has combined the best of both worlds and has enabled the equestrian ideals of the Institute of the Horse to be preserved and to be propagated to a new generation of horsemen and women.

The most obvious sign of this fortunate union—and by and large it *is* a fortunate union—is the universal use of that magic but much misunderstood word—"dressage". It is a far cry indeed from the hunting friend of the late Horace Smith, who when asked if he was going to Badminton just after that event had been inaugurated, said: "What—go and watch all those people *teasing* their horses? I've spent most of my life making my horses go forwards, not sideways and backwards!" Now I have heard even hunting people talk about dressage, and I have noticed more and more hunting people sitting deep in the saddle and not back on the cantle, which—truth to tell—is far more comfortable!

So the influence of the old Institute of the Horse, much improved and up to date, has brought the specialist branches of equestrianism in these islands to a very high standard indeed. Our top show jumpers are equal to the world's best. Our horse-trials performers dominated the international scene for a number of years, and are still a force to be reckoned with. In dressage pure and simple, which at its best is the supreme manifestation of the equestrian art, and so long a European preserve, we are knocking at the door. It is only a matter of time before some of our young riders reach the top; though I have a theory that they will not do it on English thoroughbred or three-quarter bred animals, these being in my opinion too independent-minded and self-willed for the ultimate and complete submission demanded of the super-dressage horse.

But riders of this level are naturally few in number. The British Dressage Group within the British Horse Society numbers just under 600 members, the Combined Training Group about the same; impressive indeed, but a tiny minority compared with the 12,000 membership of the whole Society. Once again we face the fact that those peaks of horsemanship—show jumping, dressage and combined training which draw the crowds and hold vast television audiences—are supported by the broad, solid base of the week-end rider. Behind them for good measure is the thirty-thousand-strong membership of the Pony Club, the great reservoir from which so many of our best riders have come in recent years. This is the situation that was unheard of, undreamt of, sixty years ago.

First it was the riding schools which catered for the new desire of working girls and men to get on horses' backs. The late Horace Smith, whose career accurately reflects the transition from the old and new times, records in his book, *A Horseman through Six Reigns* (Odhams, 1955), how in 1919, "realising that the harness age was finished", he decided to open up riding and hunting stables in various parts of the country—and did very well too. His manager at the first Maidenhead stable, incidentally, was Vincent Francis, the father of the jockey-author, Dick Francis.

That was the start of the new era, symbolised perhaps by that quartet of great riding masters and horsemen of the old school, Horace Smith, in London and Berkshire; Harry Faudel-Phillips in Essex; Jack Hance at Malvern, where he opened the first-ever residential riding school; and Sam Marsh—"Keep the tambourine a'rollin'" at Scamperdale in Sussex. They had many followers, of course, but I think no one will disagree that they had the greatest influence on riding and showing between the wars, preparing the way for the boom that was to come.

At first the clients were mostly young society people, who, again to quote Horace Smith, only "wished to learn to ride as merely an adjunct to other and varied accomplishments, and not as the be-all and end-all of life". They were happy to ride in show classes and to go well to hounds; beyond that there was little competitive riding outside the Army; the British Show Jumping Association was still in its infancy, the Pony Club not thought of.

Of course there were other instructional establishments in existence before 1919, and one most worthy of record—and perhaps the most significant, in that it heralded the female invasion of what was hitherto very much a man's world—is the riding school at Metchley, in Warwickshire, started by Miss Marjorie Avis Bullows, later to be universally known as the Lady Wright. Many successful women riders went through her school, and she herself led the way in show jumping, beating the men at their own game, much to their annoyance at first, although Tommy Glencross and Fred Foster gave her a generous welcome.

After the financial depression of 1921 the times became more prosperous, and suddenly, almost overnight, the horse was discovered by "the million". The crave to ride reached its peak in the early 'thirties, so that Reggie Summerhays could write in his first editorial in the new magazine, *Riding*, in June, 1936, "Throughout the country, people have been climbing into the saddle, often people who had never ridden before, taking it up in greatly increased numbers and full of enthusiasm for a pastime in which they found not only a pleasure undreamt of, but also an increase and renewal of good health. And so they came, adding to their numbers by hundreds and thousands, until today on Saturdays during the rush hours at our big stations jodhpurs may be seen mingling with the plus-fours without any of the self-consciousness of the conspicuous."

To cope with this flood the riding school business developed in a big way. Riding establishments, sometimes hiring only, sometimes instructional, sometimes both, sprang up all over the place, some good, many moderate, some very bad indeed. There was no control, and the new clientèle, straight from offices and factories, with no horsy background or training, was clueless as to the requirements of a properly-conducted riding school or of the needs of the horses it rode. The modern rider may have exchanged his bicycle for a horse, but he really did not see the difference.

The National Horse Association, which had been founded in 1925, mainly by Harry Faudel-Phillips, and of which R. A. Brown, recently retired from the secretaryship of the British Horse Society, was first secretary, instituted an inspection and approval scheme, and the badge of the horse's head in a horse shoe became a familiar sight on the name boards of all the best establishments. But it did not reach far enough; approval schemes never do. A general demand for the closer control of all riding schools led to the drafting of the Riding Establishments Bill in 1939, the principal object of which was to make registration of schools by local authorities compulsory and open to inspection at any time. The Bill duly got before Parliament and became law, but unfortunately in the process, for reasons not even remotely connected with the horse, its teeth were all drawn, and it emerged and still remains as a useless and unworkable Act.

World War II interrupted all these activities, though curiously enough in its later stages the interest in show jumping grew out of all recognition, leading to the post-war tidal wave of enthusiasm for the sport, which has not yet spent itself. Most of the between-wars riding schools, except for the well-established ones, had disappeared, but the still unsatiated demand soon produced new ones good and bad, which eventually brought about the same situation as in 1939. A growing agitation for action to control bad riding schools resulted at last in a new Bill, containing the all-important clauses of registration and inspection, being put before Parliament early in 1964.

There was a happy side to the situation, however, in that there were many more good places about and the standard of instruction was steadily rising, based more and more on classical principles of equitation. There was Captain Edy Goldman in Cheshire, Swiss international rider and one of the outstanding instructors of his time. There was the late Tony Collings at Porlock, where the first Olympic three-day-event teams were trained, and many others. In 1954 I wrote to a number of the leading riding masters, of whom about 40 came to a meeting at 17 Devonshire Street, London, W.1, to form the Association of British Riding Schools with the objects of raising the standards of teaching and management for the benefit of the riding school client and the riding school horse. There are now about 300 members, a small proportion still of the 2000 known establishments of all kinds, but nevertheless a useful step forward.

The next development after the last war was the riding club. A few had existed before, notably the Snaresbrook Riding Fellowship in East London and the Civil Service Riding Club, which was founded in 1939; but the big expansion occurred later.

Most of them grew naturally out of the riding school, especially those which had good tack rooms or suitable premises where riders who felt socially inclined could meet. Their members represented the best of the week-end riders, not necessarily all horse owners; urban clubs usually had to hire horses for their rallies and competitions.

The standard of riders and horses was not high, so they had no chance in open competition with professional showmen; but they were dedicated men and women and they plodded on, until the magazine, *Light Horse*, sponsored the first national event for the week-end rider in the shape of the Weekend-Riders' Rally at Iver Heath on 20 June, 1953. This was the brainchild of Walter Lorch of the Evreham Riding Club, and it took the form of a one-day event—of a sort. It was open only to those who had not won more than £3 in ordinary shows or events. The main object was to get everybody round, so that there were no eliminations, riders going on to the next obstacle and losing penalties; there were no bonus marks for speed, but penalties for overtime; the show jumping was judged on style was well as faults; the riding test was called a "control and guidance" test, and was carried out by rides of four or five, doing the simplest of movements; there was no preliminary "walking the course", the obstacles being all small and straightforward. There were 45 entries. The following year there were 90, and subsequently they had to be kept limited to about 110. It was all done on a shoe-string, but a good time was had by all.

About the same time the British Horse Society formed the Riding Clubs Advisory Committee to which all clubs were invited to affiliate. They gained many privileges and advantages, not the least being status and official recognition. There were 165 member clubs in 1963, with new clubs coming into being almost weekly. At the most conservative estimate this must mean about 15,000 riders. Behind them will be the clients of riding schools, and the pony trekkers, whose numbers must top six figures. "Riding for the Million" is not such an unlikely title for this article as it might have appeared at first.

Many of these have no interest whatsoever in equitation as such; all they want to do is to take horse exercise, to lark about and enjoy themselves. And why shouldn't they? But in their own interests and in those of the horse they need both education and some regulation—hence the Riding Establishments Act—but taken altogether they have collectively saved the nonthoroughbred horse from extinction, for which all horsemen must be truly thankful.

A natural seat is the best if the horse is to keep his balance. The greater the weight of the rider and his equipment the more important it is for the horse to carry his head and neck in a natural position.

CAPRILLI

One must learn to ride subconsciously just as one drives a car.

ALVISI

Meld, winner of the Thousand Guineas, Oaks and St. Leg with her first foal, a colt by Nearco

Versatility indeed! Mrs. E. Carlsson, née Pat Moss, equally at home on a show jumper's back as at the wheel in the Monte Carlo rally

The Romance of
Show Jumping

CAPTAIN G. H. S. WEBBER

FOR CENTURIES the horse has been the friend and servant of man. He has helped to win wars, has been the most important form of transport and has been a companion in sport.

In the early days, whether in battles or sport, it was not necessary for the horse to jump except perhaps a ditch or a small bank; but with the passing of the Enclosure Act in the eighteenth century the position changed. It was no longer possible to ride across country without jumping, and the rider soon realised how well the horse could jump and the thrill to be obtained from this new form of riding.

The birth of show jumping took place in 1866 when a class for show jumpers was arranged at a harness show in Paris. After parading in the ring the competitors were sent out to jump a few natural obstacles in the country. This was of little or no interest to spectators, and it was soon arranged that there should be a few simple fences built in the arena. Some fifteen years later the sport came to England, and by 1900 "Leaping" or "Lepping" competitions took place at the more important shows.

In 1912 equestrian events, one of which was show jumping, were introduced into the Olympic Games. At that time each country had its own rules for judging jumping, and in order to standardise this an International Federation was formed. In Great Britain there were no standard rules and each show had its own system of marking, including the award of marks for style. This led to considerable dissatisfaction and many arguments. Finally, about 1921, a meeting was arranged and attended by a number of Army officers and civilians who formed the British Show Jumping Association. This meeting took place at Olympia on the occasion of the International Horse Show which had been running as an annual event since 1907, with the exception of the war years. Throughout these early years the main jumping competition was a team one for officers representing their country, and they competed for the King Edward VII Cup, which was won outright by the Russian team in 1914.

When the show was re-started after the war this Cup was replaced by one given by Edward, Prince of Wales, and this is the trophy competed for by teams today, having been won outright by Great Britain in 1928 and re-presented by the Army Council for perpetual competition.

In 1910 King George V presented a Challenge Cup for individual competition which was won outright by Lieut. J. A. Talbot-Ponsonby in 1934 and re-presented by him for perpetual competition. These two competitions are now probably the most sought-after awards for show jumping today. There is a romantic story attached to the King's Cup. It was won in 1939 by Count Alessandro Bettoni of Italy and taken by him to his home country. During the advance of British troops through Italy, this cup was recognised in an Italian Army Officers' Mess. It was taken and eventually returned to Great Britain in the diplomatic bag. Being "pre-war", the trophy is of solid gold and would be quite irreplaceable. Now if it is won by a rider from abroad it is sent to the Embassy in London and is not allowed to leave this country.

The British Show Jumping Association became incorporated in 1925, and much was done to standardise rules and to protect the competitor from unfair and unjust decisions made by judges. In those days the stress was on standardisation and the suppression of unreasonable obstacles in order to protect the interests of the competitor. Today things have passed through a complete cycle and all the emphasis is on variety and added entertainment value. To begin with, the new Association made great progress, and the lot of the jumping competitor was much improved. However, apathy was allowed to step in and the enthusiasm for the sport died down. There was lack of interest, no variety of course or competition and, worst of all, the jumping was nearly always the last event held when all spectators had gone and only the real enthusiasts remained to compete.

At this stage the Second World War broke out and show jumping, which had made such a promising start, reverted to the doldrums, though on this occasion it was because of circumstances over which the Association could have no control.

The Romance of Show Jumping

Fortunately a few of the older and keener members kept the Association alive, and towards the end of the war, with the shortage of petrol and depleted rail services, the "Holidays at Home" movement was initiated, many country villages conceived the idea of putting on Saturday-afternoon gymkhanas, most of which included some jumping. This proved very popular, and interest in show jumping was revived.

In 1945 what is now known to have been the turning point in the sport occurred when Colonel Mike Ansell, who had been severely wounded and taken prisoner at St. Valery early in the war, was re-patriated and persuaded to renew his interest in jumping and to accept office as Chairman. During his long years as a prisoner of war, he had compared show jumping in England with his experiences of show jumping abroad and had discussed with his friend Lieut.-Colonel Nat Kindersley, who was a fellow prisoner, what was required to put British show jumping on the map as a major horse sport. Now was his chance to put these ideas into practice, and from 1945 onwards the theme has been "progress" and the improvement of the sport to make it more fun for the competitor and more entertaining for the spectator. Registration of horses, recording of results and grading of novices all played their part, and there was a definite increase in interest, culminating in the holding of the first B.S.J.A. Championship at the White City in 1946.

The course for this was designed by Mike Ansell and, by comparison with anything before it, was revolutionary. The old wings, which interfered to such an extent with the spectators' view of the jumping, were gone, and the whole aspect called forth much comment from competitors walking the course, though admittedly the remarks were made *sotto voce*. The competition was a tremendous success and turned out to be very romantic as well. It was won by Nat Kindersley riding Maguire, who, almost the last to go, jumped the only clear round. Surely this was even more than the planners in the prisoner of war camp could have foreseen, especially as Maguire, an Army horse, had been sold by auction during the war, bought by Mrs. Kindersley whilst her husband was a prisoner of war and looked after by her until his return. Ted Williams, who had been show jumping since he was very young, rode three horses to take the next three awards, a very remarkable performance. Show jumping was off to a very good re-start and the campaign to popularise it was under way. Nat Kindersley's return to win the first championship was romance indeed.

A further stimulus was provided by the fact that London was allocated the Olympic Games in 1948, and the B.S.J.A. were determined that Great Britain should be adequately represented in the show jumping. To achieve this it was clear to those few with pre-war international jumping experience that British competitors must go abroad and meet the foreigner on his own ground and under his own rules.

In 1947 a team consisting of Lieut.-Colonel Harry Llewellyn, Mr. Bobbie Hall, Mr. Tom Brake, Mr. Curly Beard and Mr. Bay Lane was selected to compete at Nice and in Rome under the management of Lieut.-Colonel Joe Dudgeon, than whom no British competitor had greater experience. Mr. Bay Lane could manage only Nice Show and returned home before Rome. Little success was achieved at first, but these riders, all first class all-round horsemen, were quick to realise what was required and smiled to themselves when they overheard the authorities at Nice discussing what they could do to enable Great Britain to win a Rosette! Had the authorities known, there was not long to wait for the answer. In Rome Harry Llewellyn registered Great Britain's first individual win abroad by winning the high jump with Kilgeddin.

At the International Horse Show at the White City in London, the individual championship of the show, the *Daily Mail* Cup, was won by a young farmer, Brian Butler, riding a thorough-bred English horse, Tankard, against strong foreign opposition in very bad weather conditions. Two years later Brian was to achieve the unique distinction of having the only two clear rounds in the King's Cup on his two horses, declaring Tankard as the winner. Great Britain was now really coming into the picture and public interest was stimulated by international competition. A third memorable event was when Great Britain won the Aga Khan Trophy at the Dublin Horse Show in 1947. In those days the competition was still confined to military teams, and Great Britain was represented by three Army officers from Germany—Lieut.-Colonel A. B. J. Scott, Major A. Carr, both from the 5th Royal Inniskilling Dragoon Guards, and Lieut.-Colonel H. M. V. Nicoll, Royal Horse Artillery. They were mounted on "liberated" German horses, and their win was quite unexpected as the best teams in Europe were competing.

Looking back, these three achievements undoubtedly laid the foundation of the popularity of show jumping.

In August 1947 another civilian team went to Ostend and Le Zoute shows, and this included, in addition to Tankard and others, Pat Smythe with Finality and Harry Llewellyn with a new horse, Foxhunter, names which were to go right to the top in show jumping.

A hard winter of training, followed by a short spell of show jumping, brought the British team Bronze Medals at Wembley in 1948 against a big entry from all over the world. The arrangements and course for the show jumping at the Olympic Games were delegated to Colonel Ansell and his B.S.J.A. Committee. The arena at Wembley did not become available for the

David Broome riding the late Sunsalve—the mo
exciting of all post-war combinations

building of the course until 9.30 p.m. on the Friday, and had to be ready for inspection by the technical delegates by 9.30 a.m. on the Saturday. Owing to the state of the ground from heavy rain it was decided that all jump material must be carried in by hand, to say nothing of the digging of a water jump and two ditches. A party of volunteers assisted by a few of the Wembley permanent staff worked all night to have the course ready on time. A capacity crowd filled Wembley for the show jumping and the closing ceremony, and many new friends for show jumping were made, thanks to the excellent organisation and spectacle.

From 1948 to 1952, the years leading up to the next Olympic Games in Helsinki, saw an amazing advance in show jumping, and Great Britain became a force to be reckoned with at international shows everywhere. Careful plans were made for the selection and training of a team for Helsinki culminating in Great Britain winning the show jumping gold medal. The team consisting of Lieut.-Colonel Harry Llewellyn and Foxhunter, Mr. Wilf White and Nizefela, and Lieut.-Colonel Duggie Stewart with Aherlow was undoubtedly the best that had ever represented this country. This brought tremendous prestige, especially as it was the only gold medal won by Great Britain at Helsinki. The national press began to recognise show jumping as a popular sport and gave it a little space in the sports columns. The Membership of the Association increased enormously and went from 500 in 1945 to over 5,000 in 1953. The interest of the general public had been won over, and television regarded show jumping as a "must" for their programmes. The advantage was mutual in that television opened up the sport to an enormous audience and in return they found show jumping a very satisfactory sport to televise. It was exciting and spectacular; the rules were easy to understand; it ran on time and, being confined to a comparatively small area, was easy and inexpensive to present.

Great Britain continued to maintain her position as a major competitor in Europe and also in the U.S.A. and Canada. Harry Llewellyn became the leading rider in Europe three years in succession. The brilliance of Foxhunter, who was equally reliable jumping-off against the clock as he was going at a normal speed, won practically every Grand Prix in Europe, and, at the same time, Harry Llewellyn had one of the finest speed horses in Mr. Eddy Broad's Monty. The combination of this fine horseman with his first class horses swept all before them. At the same time Pat Smythe, who had been a little in the background of very big competitions because of the international rule that ladies could not ride in Nations' Cup teams or the Olympic Games, was making a great name for herself and helping to popularise the sport. It was not long before she was as well known and well received at almost every European Horse Show as she is at home, and what a splendid

Who's got my bottom plate?

representative she has been. Learning to speak several foreign languages she has got the most out of her visits abroad and has been a tremendous credit to this country. Although she is now married and will spend a good deal of her time in Switzerland, she still maintains her house in Gloucestershire, where no doubt there will always be some horses.

Another great stand-by for Great Britain was Wilf White with his incomparable Nizefela. Wilf did not win many individual competitions, but he was a member of almost every winning British team and earned, most deservedly, the nickname of "England's full back". Seldom can there have been a more consistent rider and horse combination, and they made a very real contribution to British successes.

And so to 1956 when the equestrian events for the Olympic Games were held in Stockholm. Here Great Britain had considerable success. Although the show jumping team had to be satisfied with Bronze Medals, a record was created whereby Great Britain was the first country to win an Olympic Team Show Jumping Medal three times in succession. The team consisted of Wilf White and Nizefela, Pat Smythe and Flanagan and Peter Robeson and Scorchin. Peter had been a regular member of the British Team, and still is. He is a great stylist and the rider on whom one hopes our juniors will model themselves. He had been our reserve rider for the 1952 Olympic Team and, with his gallant little Craven A, a regular contributor to our international effort.

The Three-day Event team, which included Her Majesty's horse Countryman, won the Gold Medals, and the whole visit to Stockholm was enhanced by the presence of Her Majesty The Queen and the Duke of Edinburgh, who took a tremendous interest in the Games and especially in the British teams.

The B.S.J.A. has always appreciated the need for a good reserve of horses and riders and a wide base from which selection for teams can be made. With this in view it was decided that Great Britain should be represented in the European Junior championships, although the conditions for these are different from those applying in this country. Our juniors are under sixteen, whereas under international rules a junior remains such until his/her eighteenth birthday and, of course, they all ride horses of any height. Despite this disadvantage Great Britain has competed every year for the last eight and has won it seven times. A great deal of credit for this must be given to Whitbread's Brewery, who have helped to an enormous extent by providing money towards the cost of training young potential international riders under the Whitbread Scholarship Scheme, and have also contributed handsomely towards the cost of sending the British Team each year to compete. Our two European Champions David Broome and David Barker have both benefited from the Whitbread Scholarship scheme.

The Romance of Show Jumping

At the Rome Olympics in 1960 Great Britain had a set-back as the show jumping team was eliminated owing to three refusals by David Barker on Franco and the Three-day Event team failed to get a medal. Show jumping was, however, upheld by the winning of the Individual Bronze Medal by David Broome on Mr. Anderson's spectacular jumper Sunsalve, and so Great Britain did not return entirely empty-handed. However, it was immediately decided that efforts must be redoubled to produce a winning team for Tokyo in 1964, and the international programme was stepped up. In 1961 Great Britain was in the unique position of having all three European Champions, and her record in the Ladies' Championship is nearly as good as in the Junior, having won it six times in the last seven years, four times by Pat Smythe and once each by Susan Cohen (Welch) and Ann Townsend. David Broome won the Men's Championship in 1961 on Sunsalve, David Barker in 1962 on Mister Softee, and Harvey Smith was third in 1963.

Also in 1963 Great Britain won four nations' cup competitions.

Surely this has been a wonderful twenty years for Colonel Mike Ansell, whose hand has been at the helm of the B.S.J.A. throughout. He has seen the Association advance from very small beginnings to its present status in the horse world. Starting with the finding of the King George V Cup in an Italian Mess; Nat Kindersley's return in time to win the first B.S.J.A. Championship planned in a prisoner of war camp; the winning of the Aga Khan Trophy on captured German horses; Brian Butler's winning of the *Daily Mail* Cup; the winning of Great Britain's only Gold Medal at Helsinki; medals at every Olympic Games since 1948.

A romantic story? *I* think so!

TAKEN INTO PARTNERSHIP

The horse has ceased to be man's servant and become instead man's companion. In this new status the horse still has much to give us. We value his partnership as never before. Perhaps in this mechanised world of rush we strive to find an anchor with the past when we go out to ride or to school a horse in a field.

LIEUT.-COLONEL M. P. ANSELL,
in a speech before the
International Horse Show

Polo Yesterday and Today

MAJOR JOHN BOARD

IF ANY PROOF is required of the inherent resilience of the English, surely the post-war recovery of such sports and pastimes as hunting and polo provides it? And especially polo, that "millionaires' game", as it has been falsely described with one of the many half-truths which so often pass for established fact.

Admittedly, polo could not flourish without the backing of some very rich men—any more than could Racing—but, in fact, few really rich men have excelled in English polo, in the same way that they have done, for instance, in India, where some of the native princes have reached a high international standard. In England it has been a case of the rich men, such as Count Johnny de Madre, Lord Wimborne, Sir Harold Wernher and Captain Jack Harrison, mounting and maintaining the top notchers so that they might themselves have the pleasure of playing in first class company. Polo has also been described as "a game played by peers on the far side of the ground". But, up to 1939, it was the Army which more or less kept the game going in this country.

That polo should have survived triumphantly the cataclysm of the Second German War is something of a miracle. *"Ce n'est que le premier pas qui coute"* may be a true saying; and, if it is, the game owes its present prosperity—indeed, its very existence and its future promise—to the handful of pig-headed optimists of both sexes who began again in 1946 (often they had to rest their only pony, grass-fed at that, between chukkas and seldom could raise four a side) on the narrow strip of field behind Loftus Storey's house on Ham Common, and to the County Polo Association

High in the hills of Ura

under the leadership of Sidney Mason, who somehow collected an exiguous "recovery fund" to help get things going once more. It was soon after this that Lord Cowdray, who had been non-playing captain of our 1939 team at Meadow Brook and was quite undeterred by the loss of an arm during the war, reopened the House Ground in Cowdray Park.

Ever since 1948, Cowdray Park, where each July we see the best polo on this side of the Atlantic, and many of the world's greatest players, has been the headquarters of the game in England. Thanks to the imagination of Lord Cowdray, and the assistance of a running commentary, the public has been enabled to come to see polo, and to enjoy it, which was never possible in the old London seasons. More than that, they have made their own contribution to the game, through the modest charges levied for parking cars and the sale of programmes. Naturally, the keen participation of the Duke of Edinburgh and the enthusiastic interest displayed by the Queen herself—especially since the formation of the Household Brigade Club on Smith's Lawn in Windsor Park—have helped to attract large crowds on Sunday afternoons during the season.

The trouble about polo in England, from an international standpoint, is that it has always been regarded as a suitable pastime for the young gentleman of sporting proclivities, "the gun-poking, ferret-pettin', suckin' Facey Romford" of R.K.'s strictures, rather than the ideal game for the young man who is a natural ball-games player with a *penchant* towards equestrianism. The "grooved swing" is as important in polo as it is in golf. It is fairly easy to teach a natural ball-games player to ride well enough to play polo, if he has the will to learn. But if he is not the possessor of an "eye"—that indefinable coordination of mind, nerve, wrist and foot—it is practically impossible.

Our educational system has hitherto precluded the entry of promising youngsters into the game until—at least from the American point of view—they have one foot in the grave. At school they are busy with cricket and similar sporting activities, which are carried on into the holidays. So the young man who is lucky enough to be able to play polo has usually to wait until he has joined a regiment, or been otherwise emancipated, before he takes his first steps. And by that time he has probably been irretrievably committed to some other game. Fortunately, and not a moment too soon, we now have the Pony Clubs—a few of them, that is—undertaking what should have been begun forty years ago. Both the Cowdray and the V.W.H. (Earl Bathurst's), I am glad to say, have shown us distinctly promising form of late. And, what is perhaps even more to the point, Jack Meyer's rather unusual establishment in Somerset, Millfield School, includes polo in its games curriculum under

At Kopriva in the Struma valley

the direction of Roy Hern. By the time they are due to leave, a dozen or more of these boys are generally playing quite a useful game. Winchester, too, that repository of "effete" tradition and "notions", has recently permitted a pupil to absent himself at week-ends in order to play polo at Cowdray; and there seems no earthly reason why Eton and Wellington—with Windsor and Aldershot almost on their doorsteps—should not follow suit. Years ago some of us used to haunt the Wellington grounds at Crowthorne—now Wellington's "Derby Field", and given over to the legitimate pastimes of an English school—when we should have been otherwise employed.

For a multiplicity of reasons, one of the most cogent being the sundry effects of the First German War, my own polo career ended almost before it began, though not before an enthusiasm that has lasted a lifetime had been engendered. But, after fifteen years, during which time I hardly got on a horse, I returned to my first love, over a quarter of a century ago, if only as a recorder of events when I became the polo correspondent of *The Times*, which I had already served in various capacities for a dozen years. It is said that the incompetent novelist and playwright turns instinctively to criticism, and I suppose the same principle can be applied to other forms of endeavour. Up to the second war, I had a whale of a time, which included two trips *en prince* to the United States to cover the impending Westchester Cup series of 1939. There were, too, regular visits to Le Touquet, where the high life and sumptuous food provided at the Westminster, the Hermitage and the Casino were just the thing to restore a tired "special writer". Occasional paper-chases among the sand dunes, and regular rounds of golf over those two superb links, gave purpose to the mornings, as well as a ravenous appetite for the luscious luncheons, to be followed, after the *siesta*, by polo on the grounds down by the Canche. Sometimes, of course, the excessively late hours at the Casino became a bore; as did, emphatically, the daily sessions of sweating in the telephone box as I told the tale to "Auntie" over a vile line, while others were happily swilling champagne cocktails.

It all seems very far away now. And so do those other events which I have been fortunate enough to witness, and which have provided me with so many happy recollections of polo in out-of-the-way places. As for instance Diyatalawa, high in the hills of Uva in Ceylon, later at Kopriva in the Struma Valley and at Lahana on the Seres road. The years between the wars saw the high-water mark of the game in its Western development, with the United States able to mount their magnificent players on the pick of the world's ponies, and the Argentines creeping up on them.

But however unfavourably our present playing standard may compare

Gonzalez, the "player of the season," 1963

with that between the wars, though that is gradually improving, there is no doubt about the ponies. The best are as good as they used to be and on average, right through every string I have known since the war—and that must comprise several hundred, at the lowest count—the ponies of today are definitely superior. The reason is not far to seek. Although prices have not risen commensurately with the increase of other commodities, the cost of keeping polo ponies, along with the wages that have to be paid, has rocketed; so that now Mr. Jorrocks's "young Spooney" naturally buys the best that he can afford, whether from England, Argentina or Australia, irrespective as to whether or not he can hope to ride even one side of his new-found pride and joy. And I would be the last to blame him. The bad 'uns eat as much as the good 'uns, and sometimes more, cost vastly more in veterinary fees, schooling, nursing, loss of face, temper and general enjoyment. Moreover, they give little pleasure to contemplate or bestride; and they are hard to get rid of, except to the kennels—"a very expensive way to feed lions", as the *paterfamilias* of the zoo story observed. All the same, we do desperately miss the dependable, moderate-priced educated "dobbins", such as Stanley Deed used to bring over in good quantities from the Argentine each year before the war.

And this is the place, if the reader will bear with me, for a short history lesson. Up to 1914, England, being the fortunate possessor of eleven separate breeds of pony from which to choose and experiment—Exmoor, Dartmoor, Welsh, Welsh cob, Fell, Dale, Highland, Western Island, Shetland, Connemara, New Forest, to say nothing of the Galloway and Norfolk—had a virtual monopoly, infringed only by the Arab horse in his various manifestations, the country, or stud-bred Indian, and the Australian Waler. There were at least half a dozen breeding establishments along the Welsh Marches, and a fair number of others as well.

I wonder how many of the people who today support and enjoy the classes and specialist shows held under the auspices of the National Pony Society know that this Society owes its inception entirely to polo, and the need for suitable ponies to be bred; and that the lessons of the South African War had taught us (much too late) the value of mounted infantry and the type of animal suitable to carry them.

The abolition of the 14·2 limit was a quick one, perpetrated by the Americans in 1916, when we were otherwise engaged. I am sure I am not alone in mourning that abolition, and maintaining that polo on 14·2 ponies was more enjoyable, more skilful, and more favourable to well-practised tactics—as was demonstrated in spectacular fashion by the Durham Light Infantry, under the inspired and dynamic leadership of Captain (later General Sir) Beauvoir de Lisle in India about the turn of the century.

The "Young Guard": Sinclair Hill (8) No. 3 and Paul Withers (6)—leading players in the 1963 season, with a remarkable understanding between them

Polo Yesterday and Today

It was here that Argentina and the United States came in, with their small native *Criollo* Spanish stock, "improved", in the first instance, by imported English thoroughbred blood and, in the second, by the well-bred American, the Morgan, and "quarter-horse" blood of the famous King Ranch in Texas. It was at that time, in 1926 to be precise, that the world's record price of $22,000 (£5,000 then) was paid for Lewis Lacey's Argentine pony Jupiter by "Laddie" Sanford.

"A positive nuisance of recent years"

The price of a really first-class polo pony would now be around 1,000 guineas. Today there is increasing recourse to our own thoroughbreds, to be seen at reasonable prices at the Newmarket and Ascot sales; not quite fast enough for racing, but quite fast enough for polo. The best of them can hold their own against all opposition. But it is not easy to find the men to "make" them, or those who will do them justice after they are made. To be sure, we still have Harold Freeborn with Lord Cowdray; and Clem Barton, and Jack Downes of the White Stud. But such men as these are becoming pretty thin on the ground, and are likely to become scarcer.

Although the high-class animal today commands a good price, breeding ponies is no longer a profitable enterprise, save for the enthusiast who is sufficiently well heeled to do without a quick turnover. A notable example

Polo Yesterday and Today

of such a man is Mike Holden White, an American who now lives in England and who, not being able to play polo any longer, contents himself with mounting talented youngsters on ponies of his own breeding from established and brilliant playing mares, in which can be found thoroughbred, half-bred and Texan quarter-horse blood. If, as I believe, it is the dam line, as in fox-hounds, that really counts, these are practically the only "polo-bred" animals in the game today.

But the main source today is the Argentine, where there is space, low wages, cheap keep, ideal feed and, indeed, every kind of encouragement for mass production. Those that make the grade make the money; and those who do not go on the scrap-heap, or to the *gauchos* on the *estancias* or, not improbably, into the can. The well-known, world-famed breeders of the Argentine are in a position to maintain a steady distribution of high-class playing ponies, even if the fantastic cost of shipping today rules out the introduction into England of the educated but moderate animal which is such a perfect mount for the beginner.

It has to be admitted that, nowadays, there is no money in polo. But, thank God, there is still the devil of a lot of fun.

ON THE PLAYING FIELDS—BUT NOT OF ETON
Perhaps no sport tends to combine all these lessons so much as polo, none makes a man more a man than this entrancing game, none fits him more for the sterner joys of war or enables him better to bear his part in the battle of life. Pluck, endurance, submission to discipline, good temper, calmness, judgment, quickness of observation, self-control, are all qualities as essential in a good polo player as in a good soldier; and last, but no means least, there is no finer school in which to acquire the art of riding.

POLO (*Badminton Library*)

PLAIN WORDS FROM THE PAST
Certain reputations have become legendary. "Sir," said the subaltern, on receiving his first tick-off on his first day in a new country, "having been sworn at both by Henry Selby-Lowndes and George Evans, your remarks are but the twittering of a little bird." Such, indeed, is fame.

RALPH GREAVES
THE FIELD

On Dressing to go Hunting

BY A GRANDMOTHER

Some people stop hunting because they get tired,
Or they think they're too old, or their nerve has expired,
But when I give it up I will hazard a guess
It will be in connection with matters of dress.
The worst thing about hunting, to me, without doubt,
Is the business of dressing myself to go out,
It takes patience, and strength, and a great deal of time,
And before I have finished, I'll have run out of rhyme.

First I drag on a corset to hold up my back,
Which, without its support, might collapse with a crack,
Then I cover my top with a thick woollen vest,
While ankle length pants protect most of the rest.
Next I haul up my breeches to find myself faced
With the problem of how I shall fasten the waist:
I pull it together, but I never can quite
Do up the top buttons, for alas! it's too tight.
Still somehow I fix it by dint of brute force,
Praying nothing will burst till I'm safe on my horse.

To deal with my boots I depend on French Chalk,
Once they're on, they're so snug I can only just walk,
And now is the time when the telephone bell
Rings out its shrill summons (to what? who can tell?).

On Dressing to go Hunting

I put down the pull-ons and hop to the 'phone,
But I'm always too late and the caller has gone,
So I fasten my bootstraps and straighten my back,
And proceed with the job of the rest of the tack.

If the stock is to fold, as it should, and look right,
It has to begin, round my neck, far too tight,
And I must endure the occasional pin,
Exceeding its duties and piercing my skin.
With numerous grips I then master my hair,
Which I push in a net too coarse-textured to tear,
And crowning this horrid arrangement I pop
A black velvet hunting cap slap on the top.
My coat and my waistcoat are threadbare and old,
But they keep the warmth in, and they keep out the cold,
Last the gloves, and the spurs, and the whip, and its done,
With some cash in my pocket to pay for the fun.

And now comes the black moment when hobbling forth
I'm hit by the sting of the wind from the North,
Or a downpour of rain, with a promise of snow,
Till I ask myself, why in the world do I go?
To get soaking, and frozen, and frightened as well,
It's supposed to be pleasure, yet so often, it's Hell!

But at last breaks the day when the cold wind has dropped,
When the dark clouds have lifted, the downpour has stopped,
When the fences look black, when the soft sky is grey,
And without any doubt its a real scenting day.
Quick then, bring me my breeches, my boots, and the rest,
My pants, and my shirt, and my stock, and my vest,
Dressing may be a nightmare I can only just bear,
But I'll keep up the struggle for as long as I dare.

Hounds

CAPTAIN R. E. WALLACE, M.F.H.

THE BREEDING of good foxhounds considerably improves the delights of the chase for Master, huntsman and those in the country who walk puppies and interest themselves in their local pack; furthermore, it enhances the sport by producing hounds with the conformation to get over the ground and the nose, courage and "fox-sense" to keep close at their quarry. In an age in which progress of machines, science and chemistry have intensified the problems of hunting, the hound in many packs hunts and catches foxes in conditions that might have been deemed impossible some forty years ago.

As the pleasure of the ride diminishes with wire and intensive farming, houndwork comes to the fore, and, judging by what old Masters remember and from a study of pictures, it seems that the fashionable hound of today closely resembles the one of the second half of the last century—say, the sort of Lord Chaplin's old Blankney or the Warwickshire, who won the cups regularly at Peterborough in the 'eighties and 'nineties, and stemmed from the Lord Henry Bentinck strain. Although a Peterborough rosette is no criterion of prowess in the field, many Masters have always been influenced by the type shown there and inclined to use sires accordingly. At the present time we have the happy situation of the leading packs at the shows giving a particularly good account of themselves on hunting days, and of other packs investing in the blood and finding the benefit in the field. For this we have to thank such men as the Duke of Beaufort and Sir Peter Farquhar, Colonel Lowther, Colonel Borwick and several other distinguished friends of that wonderful hound man, Mr. Isaac Bell, who saw the dangers of the fashion both before and after the First World War—a fashion that made straightness, bone and round ribs of first importance and that sometimes sacrificed nose and tongue, and an idea of where the fox might have gone, for quick manœuvring of the pack on the grass, with horn and whipper-in fully applied.

Nowadays judges look, as many always did, for balance, quality and activity above all; they like a hound with good elbow, neither out nor tucked in under him, and like him anyway to move straight. A well-laid shoulder is essential, and a nice neck, longer on top than below, is a great help. Good wearing feet, which go in several shapes (not including big fleshy ones) are, of course, easier to judge in an old hound who manifestly has them. Ribs in depth, rather than barrel-shaped, are desirable in proportion to the size of the hound, and a strong loin and width over pin bone are as important as the elbow. Muscular second thighs and a good distance from loin to buttock help motivation very much, but there is some divergence of opinion over hocks. There have been many fast hounds with straight hocks and equally fast hounds with bent ones, well let down; cow-shaped hocks and those left well behind are a weakness.

Criticism of what has become the show sort of hound is directed in general terms against lack of substance. There has indeed been some danger of getting animals with neck and shoulder, but poor over the loin and with unsubstantial middlepieces—features that could lead to weakness and a tendency to be ready for home at two o'clock. Masters have been quick to spot this trend, while mindful that quality hounds beat cobs at all times. Then it is said that crookedness and backwardness at the knee are encouraged. Major Maurice Barclay, whose judging was second to none, maintained that the great point was that a hound should move straight, and that absolute straightness, although desirable, must not sacrifice the elbow or cause a knuckling over knee.

It is noticeable that an unentered hound that is plumb straight often goes wrong at elbow or knee later. Strong, springy pasterns very slightly back, allowing the whole sole of the foot to be on the ground, must help to avoid the straight line from shoulder to foot, which allows no margin for shock-absorbing. Underline is crabbed, but it is hard to recall a hound with decent ribs and strong loin tiring for this reason; scope is also a great advantage, the argument against cobs being relevant in both cases. Most judges would agree with the critics that a good shoulder, essential as it is, cannot excuse a poor back end. On the other hand, a poorly positioned elbow and shoulder will still be in trouble however good the motivating power behind.

The number of light-coloured hounds is noticeable. Quality certainly seems to go with white, but the colour does not come straight from Wales, as some suppose. A glimpse of the Puckeridge kennel, for instance, or at some of the old pictures reveals this. While there is considerable advantage in being able to pick up the pack running in the distance if there are a few light colours, it is difficult for a huntsman to tell his hounds apart out hunting when he has a lot of white ones. Hounds can be distinguished as much by their mannerisms and movements as by their markings, but a closely integrated pack of one colour is a problem even for those who know them. It may be fortuitous, but there seems to be an increase in top-class dark coloured hounds in the last year or so; in any case, of all the attributes required, colour is much the easiest to regulate and, incidentally, much the least important, and those who prefer the black and tan, with a modicum of white marking, may well see what they want in future years.

However handsome a foxhound is, and whatever illustrious names appear in his pedigree, he must be top-class in the field, and for that he depends on his huntsman and whippers-in. A noisy, silly staff can spoil the best in a fortnight. But, just as the fashion is for quality in the hound, it must be for quietness, patience and decisive action in the huntsman, and to match that the animal already described is well-equipped. Having been allowed to test the particular scent of the particular fox, in the particular place and at the time when he is hunting him, he will "tune in" and try to keep close to the line. When the fox turns short, he applies the brakes at once, hunts on if he can and comes back to where he last had the line. The right sort will throw his tongue on the scent immediately and produce females with deep voices. His good conformation helps him against fatigue and facilitates the concentration necessary to press two or three foxes in a day. If families of this sort of hound can be found, which are inclined to "run up" late in life, the breeder is a happy man. Some people imagine that very fast hounds, with great courage and drive, particularly bitches, are bound to go beyond the line, but a pack that does this suffers from too hasty a huntsman, over-riding, or failure to draft the ringleader. If aimless drifting follows at a check, a huntsman's job is nearly impossible.

What is the next development? The sires of Badminton, Portman and Heythrop are being very extensively used, and the bloodlines to hounds like Meynell Pageant '35 and Mr. Bell's great Godfrey '28 are somewhat congested. The Heythrop Brigand '54, with a complete tail-female outcross and the priceless ingredient of pre-potency, was welcome, and his progeny are now scattered far and wide. The black and tan Dumfries-shire Hounds containing a contribution from France, the College Valley, with their Fell cross, and the Cotley, combining College Valley with the tenacious West Country harrier, have many admirers; these packs have been bred and hunted by great experts and show fine sport. They include blood of a different breed from the existing foxhound and require careful mating. There are still hounds that have not been mixed with the so-called Welsh taint which have

Captain R. E. Wallace MFH, seen with the Heythrop hounds near Maugersbury

Here's to you, Masters! Masters of Hounds!

The Cheshire Hunt keep going in all weathers

Here they come sailing like gulls on the grass.
Running with drive that no pack can surpass.
Here they come, over the wall!

Hounds

good traits, and there is some scope for manœuvre within the current trends. It is a mistake to lose size, as it is only too easy to breed whippets; on the other hand, very big hounds are at a disadvantage, particularly with the prevalence of wire and the decrease of pure doghound packs. Let us cherish a medium-sized hound with class, activity and the ability to hunt closely at speed.

" *The time has come," the Young Man said,*
" *To talk of winter sport,*
Of horse and hound and hunting crop
And brandy drunk with port,
And whether it is best to wear
Your stirrups long or short."

An Anti-Blood Sports member
Was walking close at hand,
" *It's beastly for the fox," he said,*
" *And we will get it banned."*
The Young Man answered wearily,
" *You just don't understand."*

" *But it's wicked and it's cruel!"*
The A.B.S. man cried,
" *I've seen the foxes on the run,*
I've seen the way they died!"
" *If only," said the Young Man, " you*
Would see the other side."

" *You come from towns and cities*
Just to spoil the farmer's fun.
How would you keep the vermin down
By poison, trap or gun?
Do tell me what you recommend?"
But answer came there none.

CAROL WRIGHT

Counter Jumpers!

"LORINER" OF *HORSE AND HOUND*

IT'S A FUNNY THING, but although there can be very little doubt that it is show jumping that has been the spearhead of the revival of equestrianism in this country, it is still considered slightly non-u.

In the 'thirties show jumping was really carried on in two entirely different camps. There were civilians: Tommy Glencross, Miss Bullows (now Lady Wright), Stella Pierce (now Mrs. Carver), Fred Foster, Tom Taylor and the soldiers such as Howard Vyse, M. P. Ansell, Jack Talbot-Ponsonby, Dick Friedberger and C. H. M. Bunker.

Prior to the Second World War it was the soldiers who represented Britain as show jumpers. There were no international civilian teams. But it was, in fact, an Army team, rather than a British team. Indeed I very much doubt if the old British Show Jumping Association had much to do with the selection or with the arrangements.

Generally speaking this was so with most countries. It was just assumed that it was part of the function of the cavalry regiments to produce equestrian teams. And so it was. They had little else to do.

The lack of representative jumping, however, amongst civilians was discouraging, and show jumping in the 'thirties was a pretty desultory affair.

Came the war, and when show jumping again got into its stride at the end of the 'forties, the gap between civilian riders and cavalry-school riders quickly became more marked than ever.

The civilian riders, mostly farmers, and others in reserved occupations who had not seen war service, had made a little show jumping niche which was insular, parochial even, to say the least.

Counter Jumpers!

The cavalry boys had for the most part been stationed in Germany and other European countries and had begun to get ideas.

Over-simplifying the whole issue the cavalry boys now believed in going *forward*, and therefore leant towards the international rules and styles, speed being important; whereas the B.S.J.A. boys still believed in hooking up, and neither liked jumping fast, nor courses that were designed in such a way as to make them go on.

As international competition—stimulated undoubtedly by the London Olympic Games in 1948—was obviously an essential development if show jumping was going to survive, not surprisingly the soldier boys dominated the scene. The British Olympic Team at Wembley in 1948 consisted of Lieut.-Colonel Harry Llewellyn, Major Arthur Carr and Colonel Henry Nicoll.

In a great and most commendable effort to bridge this gap at the end of the 'forties the teams that travelled abroad representing Britain were civilian ones, and included such as G. B. Robeson (Peter's father), Wilf White and Tom Brake; and to be frank, they had a good deal more experience of competitive jumping than the soldiers: and only needed to learn to jump under international rules.

This they were slow to do, and equally the soldiers were not in all that much of a hurry to open their ranks to them.

However, at the beginning of the 'fifties their ranks were penetrated good and properly by two remarkable personalities: one equine, one human.

The equine one was that magnificent half-Shire whose heart was as great as his strength, even if his antecedents were somewhat plebeian: Nizefela, the property of Wilf White, a show jumping farmer who had been well known in show jumping circles before the war.

The human personality, of course, was Pat Smythe, the fairy-tale girl who had learnt her riding in suburbia, was as pretty as a picture, and proceeded at the White City to pound the greatest riders in the world on horses that had cost her but a tenth of what theirs had cost them.

This appealed to the public very much indeed; as did mighty Nizefela's kick-back. Nizefela, Tosca and Prince Hal were threatening the popularity of Lieut.-Colonel's mighty Foxhunter himself.

There is no doubt that had ladies been allowed to ride, Pat Smythe would have been in our victorious Helsinki team in 1952. But she had to wait another four years.

Nizefela was in the team and, of course, put up the outstanding performance not only of the British team but perhaps of the whole Olympic Games; but by a curious quirk of fate it was not the humbly-bred Nizefela, with his farmer rider, who had reached the final jump off for the individual medal—and should have won outright but for being wrongly faulted at the water in the first round—that came home the hero of the Olympic Games; but Foxhunter, ridden by the dashing Colonel, who retrieved an appalling first round just in time to notch up the gold medal with a clear at the end of the second round.

As far as the public and the British press were concerned it was Foxhunter who won the eleventh-hour Olympic gold medal, not the team, Foxhunter, Nizefela and Aherlow—one almost forgets who the third member of the team was; but she was ridden, of course, by Colonel Duggie Stewart, commanding officer of the Scots Greys; so this was indeed a triumph for the soldiers.

The rift was as wide as ever.

The B.S.J.A. in a gallant effort to prevent the gap widening appointed Wilf White, ostensibly one of the old B.S.J.A. boys, captain of Britain's international team, a role which he carried with expected modesty but with apparent discomfort, due perhaps to the feeling that he was considered something of a blackleg by his old pals.

In fact he was one of the few who had the foresight to see that international-style jumping had come to stay. International courses would be built in such a way as to make horses go *forward*. This was the obvious, if unpalatable truth. But his gesture was not altogether well accepted.

The rift now had subtly changed. It was no longer the Army that rivalled the B.S.J.A. boys, for the simple reason that the Army no longer produced horsemen. Rather it was the classicists. That is to say, it was a group of riders, mostly under thirty, with a female predominance, who, inspired by and imitating the best continental riders, under the tuition of great foreign experts or astute mentors such as the editor of this book, adopted a classical style of riding in marked contrast to the acrobatic style of riding associated with the hook-up and accelerate style now favoured by the B.S.J.A. boys.

The latter headed, of course, by such as Alan Oliver, Ted Edgar, Derek Kent, with the veteran Ted Williams as their doyen, had some formidable recruits to their ranks in the 'fifties, too.

But the classicists—or the Arundel set as they were sometimes called because of the group who received expert tuition from Colonel Talbot-Ponsonby through the perspicacity of the Duchess of Norfolk—also had some useful recruits: Anne Townsend, Sarah FitzAlan-Howard, David Barker and, of course Peter Robeson.

They were taught all the time to "go on", and great successes they achieved. In addition to which they gave great pleasure to the eye.

Poised between the two schools, with her usual detachment, was Pat Smythe, and the new bright hope of show jumping, the individualist genius, David Broome, who accepted no theories, owed allegiance to no one, but

"... the Classicists appear to have the edge on the game"
Captain Piero d'Inzeo on The Rock

Counter Jumpers!

just got up and got on; and completely caught the imagination of the public.

Socially, temperamentally, his sympathies were probably with the boys; but with his natural dash, his superb sense of timing and his wonderful hands, enabling him to ride with the lightest contact and no gadgets, his performance seemed more to line him up with the classicists.

In fact he alone came home from the Rome Olympics with an enhanced reputation. The David Barker–Franco débacle had rocked considerably the classicists' platform, whereas the boys had been left out in the cold altogether.

They wasted no time, however, in producing their own new bright hope. This was Harvey Smith, who, like David Broome, owed allegiance to no one. A natural if ever there was one, with a style all his own, a style as individual and recognisable as it was successful.

The Establishment—for this was how it was now regarded—lost no time in an attempt to win him over by providing him with a top international horse; and so while it could be said he now had a foot in each camp his seat remained independent—as independent, in fact, as his character: and although justifiably, he enjoyed the fruits of the high table, yet he was generally more at home with the boys and regarded as their spokesman.

"Harvey says——", etc.

Retaliation from the Establishment was not long delayed: and with a delightfully ironic touch, patron of their new hope was none other than the patron of Harvey Smith—Mr. Robert Hanson, that great and generous benefactor of show jumping; as shrewd as they come, too.

The new protégé, of course, was Anneli Drummond Hay, a superb horsewoman and "educated" in every sense of the word. In one season she swept to the top. Her immediate and convincing success must surely, it was thought, strengthen the Establishment and cause dismay in the ranks of the boys.

In the pre-Olympic season the rivalry was really hotted up. Some even insisted that courses were especially designed to suit one or other cause. Either they consisted of endless high upright fences, inviting the hook, the acceleration, the accuracy; or they consisted of spreads, combinations with stretching distances, demanding that the rider kept going forward, going on.

Each faction criticised with gusto courses that suited the other faction.

Through all this the general public has remained splendidly detached. The millions who watch show jumping on television have been quite content to take to their hearts a perfectionist Peter Robeson or an acrobatic Alan Oliver; anyone who could give them a thrill.

The particular public, by which I mean the *cognoscenti*, have regarded the whole affair with a certain tolerance. They are determined to be able to say

*he millions who watch television have been quite content to take
their hearts a perfectionist such as Peter Robeson*

that they were with whichever side wins, and they do still consider those who show jump as slightly non-u, especially if they do not hunt in the winter.

In fact, those who can genuinely claim to be detached have to admit that the classicists appear to have the edge on the game. In the first place the authorities have been clever enough to play down the rift, smoothing over wherever possible any obvious excesses on either side.

Secondly, more and more of those in a position to influence the situation one way or the other have become convinced that the classic style is the one likely to be most effective, especially in international jumping; and so more and more courses tend to be of the sort that invite riders to keep going on.

With the constant increase in "educated" riding, and more and more of the "thought out" approach to jumping a course, as opposed to the happy-go-lucky, meet 'em as they come approach, it would seem that victory is in sight for the classicists.

But will it, in the long run, be a hollow victory?

One does not have to be an expert to realise that the Germans now, and even the Italians, seem to have adopted a style which depends far more on hooking-up and powerful acceleration than it does on lengthening the stride and going on.

How very non-u!—especially if they beat us!

The steeplechase jockey has one evil to guard against, which the racing jockey is, comparatively, but little subject to, and this is a fall. The best preventive of it is keeping a horse well together, and making him go in a collected form at his fences, as well as over rough ground. But, at the same time, he must not overpace his horse, or he will not be able to rise at his fences when he gets to them.

CHARLES JAMES APPERLEY ("NIMROD"), 1779-1843

The horse is a living vehicle, a gift to man from nature. A horse soon knows whether his rider is a man or a beast.

A Day from Buttadoon

T. D. ROOTES

IT HAD BEEN a very hard winter in England. From Christmas until mid-February the country had been completely snowbound. An invitation from Stopper and Mumble Umberleigh-ffudge for a long weekend to hunt in Ireland was more than welcome.

A year or so before I had stayed with them for a few days in the summer, when the object of my visit had been to buy a horse. Mumble sold me a four year old she had bred, which proved a great success. She loved a "deal" and had a reputation for finding good horses. This time I told her I was looking out for a youngster to point-to-point; a bulky letter by return post described a variety of animals with pedigrees lavishly garlanded with winners. It appeared as an insoluble problem to choose from all these desirable bargains. About one she said, "He has such quality and scope that when he is the trained article in the ring at Cheltenham all England must agree this is another Mill House." At times Mumble's imagination ran riot.

The Umberleigh-ffudges' house, Carnalmather, was beautiful and un-comfortable. Outside, crumbling plaster walls; inside, fine Queen Anne and Georgian furniture, with enormous and ugly Victorian paintings. None the less a wonderful air of happiness prevailed. James, the butler, ran everything with apparent casualness but great efficiency. He also had a splendid sense of humour—necessary in a house filled with so many dogs I never knew their names. They weren't really house-trained, but Mumble was not aware of this. As the doors never seemed to be closed any faintly odd aroma eluded her.

I flew into Shannon on a Friday night. Mumble was having a dinner-party that evening; twenty for dinner, she happily informed me. Her guests

A Day from Buttadoon

arrived spasmodically, from eight till ten-thirty when we sat down to dine. Nobody seemed to mind. I was by then oblivious of time, as Stopper had filled me full of whisky and sodas since my arrival.

I was seated next to Mumble's sister, Sylvia Beauwhistle, who dominated the conversation at my end of the table. Under a deceivingly frail and attractive exterior, Sylvia possessed a tireless physique and pugnacious temperament. I believe she sang on the stage in her early youth. I imagine vocal training, aimed to fill Drury Lane, accounted for her ability to drown any conversation. She certainly holloaed more effectively and excitingly than anyone I have heard. She had successfully married the 10th Earl of Beauwhistle, in the teeth of his family's displeasure and hostility and in spite of his unaffected indifference to women. "Wanker" Beauwhistle, as his more intimate friends called him, was forty when Sylvia came into his life; after fifteen years of marriage he had wasted bodily and faded mentally into a dejected shadow loosely attached to the forthright and exacting Sylvia.

James had placed, presumably from habit, a large bottle of whisky in front of Sylvia, with which she continuously topped up our glasses. I had agreed to drink whisky with her rather than mix my drinks (Stopper's cellar was excellent), in the unlikely hope of keeping a clear head for the next day's hunting.

On my other side sat Selina Calhoune, the wife Cockburn Calhoune, an American who hunted one of the local packs. Selina I knew slightly, and I found her reticent and difficult to talk to; once a leading and beautiful debutante in Philadelphia, now many winters in Ireland and the rigours of the hunting field had taken their toll. However she took the initiative and launched into a boring discourse on what, I think, must be a detestably over-cultivated garden. My attention was maintained by watching Selina's extraordinary eyelids. They were covered with what I can only describe as sparkling 'hundreds and thousands". She emphasised her conversation with long dramatic blinks, inducing the sparkles to descend in a shower, down her dress, on her food, and finally into her coffee. As the ladies left the room Sylvia hissed, "Such a bore, Selina—everything that belongs to her is perfection—her house, garden, horses, husband, children are all superlative—no one has ever had anything like them." "If one of her rhododendrons died she would expect it to be on the news!"

Thankfully, I sat down to enjoy the safe and easy topics that seem to emerge for discussion over the port. I stumbled to bed about two-thirty, determined to get some sleep before hunting the next day.

I awoke in the morning to find James pouring out some tea by my bed. "Good morning, sir. There's a bit of a fog outside. I'm afraid it may stop them hunting." At that moment I felt nothing but relief. Tired from the

66

A Day from Buttadoon

journey the day before, and particularly by the evening, I swallowed my tea and sank back to further slumber.

Almost at once it seemed, Mumble burst into the bedroom. "Get up," she cried. "I've rung Cockburn. They're having a lawn meet at Ballypooley and he says the fog is clearing fast, so hurry up." I shaved, threw on my hunting clothes and rushed downstairs determined not to miss breakfast.

Mumble's breakfasts are marvellous. There was a lot of happy chatter going on about the prospect of the day's sport while we devoured porridge, eggs, kidneys and bacon, thick slices of home-made bread straight from the oven, and brown treacly marmalade, accompanied by quantities of tea or coffee. I had barely finished my last mouthful when Mumble and Stopper announced that we must leave at once.

We set off from Carnalmather in two old battered Fords. The Umberleigh-ffudge's must have owned them for a decade. Driving to Ballypooley I became apprehensive about the possibility of hunting—the fog was still bad. Stopper, whose eyesight and hearing had known better days, was crawling from one side of the road to the other muttering, "Can't think how that bloody fool Cockburn thinks he can hunt in this muck—would have been much more sensible to have stayed at home and played poker."

We finally arrived at Cockburn and Selina's, only to realise that we could not possibly move off for at least an hour.

Ballypooley, a severe white Georgian house, stands in a lovely park with what is normally a beautiful view across a fine artificial lake. There were a number of horseboxes, cars and trailers parked along the drive, and a few horses led about by local lads. Cockburn rushed up to the car, "Everyone is inside: go and give yourselves some port."

The hall was crammed with an amazing assortment of people. About twenty dressed in conventional hunting clothes, and a series of variations on the basic theme. In addition there were a mass of supporters and followers, all jovially enjoying the Calhounes' hospitality.

About two hours elapsed. I found I had drunk a great deal of port and brandy. The fog spasmodically showed signs of lifting, so most people hung about in hopes. Slowly, however, hunting began to become less important. As I munched hot mincepies and talked to a large and vivacious woman with flaming red hair (now released from its normal hunting captivity), I was vaguely aware of music.

My companion pointed to a young couple vigorously twisting, With a lascivious wink and a ravishing smile she asked if I was "with it"? At that moment I realised almost everyone was dancing. Seizing my companion we joined the throng of twisters, all looking ridiculous in our hunting regalia. Someone pulled the curtains. I heard the "plop" of a champagne cork. In a

A Day from Buttadoon

dimly lit corner I saw Sylvia smoking a cigar on the lap of a wizened rather military man known as "Fruity"—what his other name was I never discovered.

Suddenly, to my astonishment, my red-headed friend, whose twisting had become quite abandoned, lay down on the floor and started what I can only imagine was supposed to be a demonstration of the breast stroke. As I gazed unbelievingly at her, Sylvia seized me by the arm and whispered, "Come with me. When Daphne starts swimming it's a sure sign of danger—then, oh! boy, you had better look out. It usually happens at three in the morning—God knows what happens at three in the afternoon." She dragged me into the kitchen where Mumble and some other women were making sandwiches. Tea and food brought us back to earth and we finally left Ballypooley about 5 o'clock. It was still foggy, I had missed a day's hunting and it did not seem to matter. Our drive back to Carnalmather was very relaxed. Stopper sang a series of bawdy barrackroom songs alternating with Sylvia's deafening renderings of "You go to my head" and "Mad about the boy".

The next day was sunny and clear. The meet was at Buttadoon, only a mile from Carnalmather. Somehow we were late and arrived to find the main street of Buttadoon alive with activity. Hounds were just moving off. Hordes of children, bicycles, cars and foot followers were preparing to follow the field. A moment of panic while Mumble failed to find Paddy, who was to produce my horse. This character was finally located lurking beside one of Buttadoon's pubs. (There were fifteen in the main street.) Paddy was holding a raw, rough-looking thoroughbred, trace clipped, with a lot of substance and a rather formidable wall-eye. I seem to remember asking nervously if the animal had a name. "Sure, he's called 'Beserk'," I was told. At least it sounded like that to me, but perhaps it was my susceptible imagination. "Didn't this feller give another English visitor the grandest ride a couple of weeks ago." Paddy warmed to his topic. "Wouldn't Father O'Donnell, who is great to go, tell you so himself, if he wasn't in hospital still unconscious from taking a terrible toss on the tarmac road—mind you, he's a brave man and the horse must have put his foot in a hole for he never fell in his life before."

With these encouraging words, I nervously seized some hard thick reins and was thrown up on a rather battered old racing saddle. At that moment Mumble came past yelling at me to follow. Her horse seemed to be progressing with great agitation sideways down the road, kicking violently every few yards. "Beserk" flew off in her wake determined, I felt, to imitate Mumble's progress.

I remember thinking as we followed in hectic pursuit of the field, that there are moments when hunting is hell. I had desperate clairvoyance that I would

The famous Scarteen (Black and Tans) hounds in full cry near Kilrush

"In the middle of the field we were held up by the Field Master whilst Shaun and the hounds worked around the banks in the next few enclosures"

Dangerous viewing!

A Day from Buttadoon

be quite incapable of controlling the wild and abandoned plunges of my over-fresh horse which seemed to suffer from a strange swerving sickness. Almost anything turned him aside from the course I was trying to induce, into a vivid imitation of forked lightening.

Mumble and I reached the first cover breathless, scarlet in the face but relieved to find the field intact. "Hogan's Gorse", it appeared, was blank, and almost at once we moved to the next cover, "Mullin's Wood". "It's a sure find," I heard on all sides.

My progress to this was not a success. "Beserk", it appeared, was continuously overcome with affection for almost any horse which came alongside him. I was therefore quite unable to talk to anyone without the brute hurling himself drunkenly into my adjacent companion. This, coupled with another impossible habit—that he frothed copiously from the mouth—made me unwelcome on all sides. In the high wind "Beserk's" frothing, like snow, quickly covered all around me. We finally arrived at "Mullin's Wood", which after all was blank.

Then the Master, Shaun O'Neil, who I had met dining the first evening, decided to draw the countryside on the way to "Ballinagad Bog". This seemed sensible: we might find an outlying fox in one of the large fluffy banks and possibly lose some of the thrusting car followers.

We came to our first obstacle, which was a large rusty sheet of corrugated iron—in a gap—with a tight strand of barbed wire six inches higher. To my astonishment "Beserk" flew across this horrible affair with such a spring that I was nearly jumped off. Almost at once we were faced with a huge double bank with a deep wide drain in front of it. I could not see over the top of the bank and it seemed almost unjumpable. However, no one was deterred and I saw half a dozen riders trot up to the ditch: some of the horses almost appeared to stop, and then suddenly would jump, landing catwise on the near vertical face of the bank, struggling to the top.

Mumble cantered up to me and said, "For God's sake don't hang around and be polite! All these people—particularly some of the women—will take advantage of a stranger and push past you, and do remember that after the banks have been jumped a few times they can collapse and become greasy and slippery." "Come on," she cried, and I followed.

To my surprise I arrived somehow onto this vast obstacle much quicker than I had anticipated—found the top of the bank narrower than I thought— "Beserk" was so quick that we were off the bank, across the enormous drain the other side, and almost collided with Mumble's horse, which had landed safely and cleverly. I shot past her, gathering reins and one of my irons.

In the middle of the field we were held up by the Field Master whilst Shaun and the hounds worked around the banks in the next few enclosures.

A Day from Buttadoon

Suddenly I was startled by a piercing shriek in a voice I thought familiar. This was Sylvia—not, in fact, holloaing a fox, but screaming with rage and fright at her horse, which was rolling ecstatically in a large, wet, muddy gap. Beside me Cockburn whispered loudly, "That's a nice change of mud for Sylvia. She is usually bathing expensively in hot bubbling mud at a Mediterranean resort devoted to the desperate pursuit of eternal beauty."

After jumping three or four more banks in cold blood, a fox was viewed away. Then ensued some of the most exciting and hair-raising moments I have ever known. Scent must have been wonderful and hounds were flying: it was every man for himself. Following Mumble's advice, I set sail at a big clean-looking bank on my own. On reaching the top, I saw to my horror what seemed to be a river on the other side. Paralysed, I desperately looked along the top of the bank to my left and right. "Beserk", however, made up my mind. Half creeping, half sliding down to the water, he got his hocks under him and with a tremendous leap landed in the field beyond.

For the next few minutes we galloped through bottomless going, the deepest I have ever encountered. Mostly the banks were narrow and steep, often with what seemed impenetrable growth on top. However, there always appeared to be someone brave enough to force a way through. We came to a railway line, where a locked iron gate had to be lifted off its hinges; madly we galloped along the line for about a mile, when the hounds continued their point by turning sharp right. This time there was no gate in sight and I was alarmed to see people taking on a barbed wire fence, half obscured with grass, and a fantastic drop to the field below .

By this time our ranks were considerably thinned out. The next bank had a large barbed wire oxer on the face of the bank, the stakes pointing towards us. Slightly out of control, and going too fast, my horse gave a great leap and with the sound of twanging wire we reached the top. In a flash I saw the same ugly sight the other side. Finding an extra leg, "Beserk" flung himself miraculously over the wire. We pitched on landing in the soft mud and I rolled off—really quite unnecessarily, and largely through exhaustion and fright. I landed on my back with a squelch, but somehow held on to the reins. I have never been agile enough to remount quickly, but now exhausted and covered in wet mud, it took me a long time to climb on to my horse's back. Luckily hounds had checked, so we had the chance to regain our wind.

Scent then seemed patchy for a few fields. Gradually the country became more undulating and the going improved. We jumped the odd stone wall; once Mumble and I were by ourselves cantering across an enclosure when we came to a small wall. It looked quite innocent. We jumped this deceiving obstacle together, when I heard a scream from Mumble and at the same time

A Day from Buttadoon

saw a huge drain the other side at least eight feet across. Again it seemed disaster was certain.

Miraculously, "Beserk", instead of flying the wall, changed in mid air as if trying to double it. With the sound of his heels clicking on the stones he just reached the far bank.

Still on rising ground, we crossed a main road. In front of us lay what might have been a small part of the Sussex Downs, rising dramatically into the skyline. It was a sudden change of scene and light, which happens unexpectedly in Ireland. Hounds were climbing a lone hill ahead. Breathlessly we watched them disappear over the skyline against the setting sun. I saw the Master and Whip dismount to climb the hill. Mumble and I followed suit.

Panting as we reached the summit, we paused and Mumble said, "My heart feels as if it will jump out of my body. I must wait here a minute."

We could see the hounds, by now about a mile away, disappearing into the fading evening light. A wonderful view. Mumble told me from that spot you can see some forty miles and no less than six counties. I gave her a leg up and our horses seemed rejuvenated after their brief rest.

Off we went again, cantering downhill and jumping walls, now smaller than before. Then we heard in front of us the sound of Shaun's horn triumphantly telling us his hounds were rewarded and had killed their gallant fox.

An hour or so later, half a dozen of us were sitting in a small pub in front of a glowing turf fire. Stopper arrived with a basket of food to help soak up the quantities of whisky which we were recklessly consuming. Later, half drunk with happiness and alcohol, I fell asleep by the fire—warm; replete, and dreaming of hunting, and hunting, and hunting. . . .

"Beserk", it transpired, was only rising four. He now lives in the best box in my yard.

It is an illusion to imagine that one can hold a horse up by pulling at the reins. I have fallen off hundreds of times and I invariably notice that I could never have avoided a toss by the use of my hands, but on the contrary, the fall was usually due to the over-use of my hands which deprived the horse of his natural power of recovery.

CAPRILLI

Behind the Scenes

LIEUT.-COLONEL JACK TALBOT-PONSONBY, D.S.O.

COMPETING in a show jumping competition entails a great deal more than simply riding into a ring, and jumping a succession of fences. The horse must be carefully trained, so that he is obedient to the rider's wishes, and so that he is capable of being balanced in order to jump any type of fence easily, and without undue effort. He must be fit, and must have had sufficient jumping practice at home to ensure that his muscles are attuned for this type of work. The rider must also be fit, so that his brain is alert, and reacts at once to any eventuality, thus being able to impart immediate instructions to his muscular system to give the required indication to his horse. He should thoroughly acquaint himself with the procedure to be followed on arrival at the show, so that every little detail is remembered, and he is not flustered or worried before entering the ring owing to some little thing having been forgotten. The training of the horse to a standard sufficiently advanced to warrant taking part in a jumping competition in public will have taken time, and will have needed considerable patience and hard work. The rider will, no doubt, have to have accepted setbacks cheerfully, both in the matter of his own methods of riding and in his horse's behaviour, but, with concentration and determination, these will have been overcome, and the time will arrive when everything is ready for participation in a jumping competition.

Method and appreciation of detail are important in all things. Show jumping is no exception to this. Horse and rider must approach their test in the ring with calm confidence, and this is very largely made possible by

The Borghese Gardens, the picturesque setting for the annual Rome International Horse Show

Aachen: the largest permanent show ground in the world, containing hazards of all types

forethought and attention to detail, before leaving home for, and upon arrival at, the show. Concentration, and the will to win, are very necessary attributes in a show ring rider, and these can quite easily be disturbed or damped by petty annoyances occurring before the commencement of a round. Such annoyances are infinitely less likely to occur if a system is adopted, so that details of preparation for the show, and procedure at it become automatic, and everything follows smoothly up to entering the ring itself.

When the time approaches for attending a show it is obviously essential to be certain that the horse's shoes are in order, that they are fitted with stud holes in the correct places, and that the selection of studs are, in fact, the right size. How often at a show the cry is heard, "My studs don't fit, has anyone got some with a different thread from these?" Stud holes are apt to become damaged, so a re-threading key is a valuable piece of equipment, and a screwing key an essential one. The stitching in saddlery wears with age, leather can tear gradually, and buckles become bent and ineffective. Boots and breeches, or jodhpurs, sometimes need repair, coats and hats need cleaning, and nothing looks worse than a scruffy appearance. Such things need looking into in sufficient time for any alterations or repairs to be carried out so that everything is ready the day before that of the show itself, and the rider himself must be certain that such is the case. The afternoon before, the route and distance to the show should be worked out, and the time for starting calculated so that the horse arrives there not less than an hour before the scheduled time for jumping. If a long distance has to be covered, it is particularly important for the horse to have a rest from the noise and movement of the box before being prepared for the ring. Remember too that horse-boxes have been known to suffer breakdowns, and it is difficult to make up lost time in that type of vehicle.

The morning of the great day dawns, and there is plenty to do at home. The horse's stomach should not be full when he goes into the ring, and so feeding must be worked out with this in view. All horses vary in the amount of exercise required before giving of their best, and the ideal amount should have been determined during practice—so it will already be known if it is advisable to work your horse at home, and if a few suitable jumps will be advantageous to him. If some work is required, carry it out early, leaving plenty of time for him to cool off and settle down before loading. Pack the saddlery carefully in the box to avoid the possibility of damage during the journey, check that each item is included, not forgetting the stud kit, and take a hay net for the trip home. Remember to put in your personal riding equipment and any tickets that may have been sent you by the show secretary, get ready yourself, load your horse into the box, and everything is prepared for the fray.

ansy fences require great accuracy:
k Talbot-Ponsonby riding Penny

Behind the Scenes

On arrival at the show ground, choose a site, if possible, where there is some shade if the weather is hot, and from which you can hope to get the box out if the ground is very wet. Then start your previously planned show routine. Ascertain if the programme is up to time, and if not, calculate to the best of your ability at what time your event should begin. If your number has not already been sent you, collect it from the secretary's tent, and in any case, inquire in what order numbers are to be taken for jumping, again if this has not already been stated. This will, unfortunately, normally entail visiting the collecting ring steward, and having your number put on his list. It is, without doubt, a great help to be sent your number and order of jumping prior to the show, but this means considerable secretarial work, and small shows can seldom manage to do it. On return to your box, get the saddlery and your own kit ready, fit the necessary screws, and, if the horse requires a practice jump before going into the ring, put up the poles carried in the box.

By this time you can reasonably expect to find a plan of the course displayed in or near the collecting ring. This is, unfortunately, not always the case. Do not hesitate, however, to ask the collecting ring steward if you may see it. A properly prepared plan will show the start and finishing points, the position of each fence in the course numbered in the order to be jumped, and so the route to be followed, the total length of the course, the speed required, the time allowed and the time limit. It will not show the type or size of the fences. The plan should be carefully studied, and the position of every fence memorised, so that, when the inspection of the course is allowed, no time will be wasted in finding the way round. As has been said, different horses require different periods of work before jumping, so saddle up and commence work at the appropriate time, ensuring that the horse is alert and in an obedient frame of mind. Everything will then be ready for the next, and extremely important item, the inspection of the course itself.

As the majority of shows wage a perpetual fight against time, it is probable that only a short period will be allowed for competitors to inspect the course. Be ready, therefore, to enter the ring as soon as permission is given. Your previous study of the plan will now stand you in good stead, as you will already know well the approximate position of each fence, and the various changes of direction.

First, then, walk quickly round the whole course by yourself, noting the exact position of each fence, the angle in which they are sited in relation to each other, and so the best line of approach and its extent. Having completed this initial survey, go round again, following the exact track you intend to take, and make a detailed study of each fence with especial reference to its type and dimensions, thereby determining the pace at which it must be approached. In the case of doubles or combination fences, measure the distance between the jumps, which will indicate the number of strides to be taken between them, and note the type of each, for this will govern the pace of the approach. For instance, if the first jump of a double is a triple bar, the pace must obviously be faster than if it were a plain gate. There is a great deal to decide in a short space of time. Do not hesitate to ask advice if in doubt on any point, but be certain that your advice comes from an authoritative source, and, having asked for it, stick to it. Finally remember that this preliminary to jumping is of the utmost importance to the success of your round, and be certain that your time for course inspection is not wasted in idle gossip with your friends, an all too common occurrence.

The stage is now set for the competition to start. It will often be a help to watch a few good riders on good horses go round, so that you can check the distances in doubles, and make certain that your calculations were correct. You can also get a general impression of how the course actually rides. For these reasons, when the order of jumping is not definitely laid down, it will be advantageous to you to have arranged your turn with the collecting ring steward so that at least six competitors are in front of you. Get mounted in plenty of time, and just before your number is called canter round to ensure that your horse is on his toes, and behaving obediently. When your turn comes, ride well into the ring, so that you have plenty of room to come round to the start at a balanced canter, and listen for the bell, the judges' indication that they are ready for you to start. Do not start until you are quite certain that the bell has sounded, for crossing the start line before entails disqualification. Now comes the test of all your training and preparation. With your plan of campaign firmly in your mind, ride calmly and with determination. Concentrate absolutely on riding the course, and let nothing interfere with this concentration. Let your eyes always follow your chosen route, and never look back. Above all, keep your horse balanced throughout.

The finishing line is passed, and you begin to take in the applause from round the ring. You hear the commentator announce, "A clear round", and you ride quietly out feeling satisfied that your plan was soundly conceived, and that your performance has been smooth and fluent. Dismount outside the ring, give your horse some little titbit to show your appreciation of his efforts, and loosen your girth. There will probably be other clear rounds, so you must now start preparing for the jump-off. Meanwhile have your horse led quietly about in hand, and do not allow him to graze. You will know from having studied the conditions of the class before the show what form the jump-off will take, the number of jump-offs to decide the winner will have been stipulated in the conditions of the class, and the course for each one will be shown on the plan, the last being, of course, on time. So study carefully the jump-off course, and again formulate your riding plan, bearing in mind that the fences will be larger, both in height and width, probably requiring a slightly longer approach. When your turn to jump comes, concentrate on concentration, ride with dash and determination, and, with fortune smiling, the prize will be won. Do not let success overshadow your sense of responsibility, but see to the welfare and comfort of your horse, the very willing collaborator in the venture. Go back to the box, unsaddle, take the screws out, remembering to plug the holes to avoid damage to the thread, and let him graze while you rub him down. If you have a long journey before you, let him wash his mouth out with some fresh water. As soon as he is settled and cool, load him up and drive home, with a nice feeling of pride in your achievement, and of quiet confidence in the future.

Taking part in a show jumping competition is not, then, simply a matter of riding into a ring and jumping a succession of fences. Apart from the training of the horse there are a thousand and one points to be remembered, thought out and acted upon, which, as a whole, will guide you along the path to success. The omission of even one small item may well cost you a competition. The emphasis, therefore, at the show must be on method and attention to detail.

NO CONSEQUENCE
"I say, Jack! Who's that come to grief in the ditch?"
"Only the parson!"
"Oh leave him there, then! He won't be wanted until next Sunday."
JOHN LEECH
THE NOBLE SCIENCE

Deprive him of horses and hounds as you will,
A fox-hunter once is a fox-hunter still.
. . . Choice of the heart's desire,
A short life in the saddle, Lord!
Not long by the fire.
LOUISE IMOGEN GURNEY

High Hopes and Hard Graft

JOHN GROSS

FIRST OF ALL I think we should explain the basic aims of a course builder; they are, to design and build jumping courses that will provide the spectacle of good jumping for the public, interesting riding for those competing, while at the same time endeavouring to produce a course that is complimentary to the type of competition, whether it be for novice horses or ponies or for those of international standard.

The course builder himself must be fully experienced in dealing with all these types of competitions; have a liking for getting soaking wet; have a skin as thick as an elephant's; and be able to survive on a basic diet of cold ham and chicken, occasionally varied to chicken and ham, for most of the summer.

Let us assume that we are engaged by the Loamshire Agricultural Society as course builder for their annual three-day show. Our first job is to ask the hard working Show Secretary for a schedule of the competitions, and if it is our first visit, details of the main ring size, position of entrance and exits and any other relevant information and also, most important, what they are having by way of ring displays.

This last item has quite an important bearing on the designing of your courses, as you must endeavour to place the most important fences where, you hope, they won't have to be moved for the display.

You are now in a position to settle down and start designing your main course incorporating into it the changes you need for subsequent competitions.

The working party has been laid on to meet you at 10 a.m. on the day prior to the show, and you make sure you arrive at the ground in good time to report to the Secretary's Office before meeting them.

A little snag now crops up; your working party consists of about half a dozen very keen, but rather small, boys plus one tractor and trailer complete with driver, for which you are extremely grateful.

The literal size of the party comes as a bit of a shock as you had visualised about a dozen hefty fellows waiting for you with all the fences already assembled in their units ready stacked in the near vicinity of the main ring, so your hopes of getting the bulk of the building completed before lunch has vanished straight away.

So let's face it, we have a few little lads, very keen, very polite, so let's get on with it.

You start by giving them a little pep talk about the importance of their job, etc., and then tell one of them to go to the stack of fence material and bring you a set of numbers so that we can start setting them out in the ring to facilitate the placing of the fence material.

After an interval of a couple of minutes the little boy comes rushing back and says, "Excuse me, sir, what fences?" and after exercising great self-control you proceed to go in search of same, only to find that they have been dumped in a pony ring which is about 250 yards from where you want to use them.

Everyone on to the trailer and off to the other ring we go where we find the fences in a heap, so we are faced with having to start the job right from scratch.

By this time the "tea break" has arrived, so you send your party off to comply with this typically English tradition, whilst you remain behind to start putting the detachable feet on to the wing stands—you don't care much for tea anyway.

After the tea break work really gets under way and your lads are working like beavers and very quickly get the hang of how the various parts of the fences go together, they also have added incentive to hurry, as by this time it is beginning to look very much like rain.

Whilst the lads are finishing off this preparatory work, you go back to the main ring and set the numbers out in the approximate position of the fences so that the material can be placed near to hand.

Back in the other ring all is ready to load up the material for the first fence; off goes the tractor and trailer with a couple of lads to unload in the main ring while you remain behind with the rest to get the next fence ready for loading.

Experience has shown that as soon as one utters the words "You two go with the tractor, please", every member of your party immediately leaps onto the trailer, and it proves to be quite a major operation to get the balance off, leaving only two to go with the load.

Ten minutes have now elapsed and no sign of the tractor returning, so you go back to the main ring to investigate, only to find your lads busily investigating the mysteries and wonders of the automatic timing set which is being set up for testing.

You marshal your flock and proceed back to the pony ring, and find that it is now lunch time, so once again you are alone and carry on sorting and loading up. You don't care much for lunch either.

Eventually all is complete; the rain did come as expected, you are all soaked to the skin, so as soon as the course is completely built you thank your gallant little army and send them off and then "go it alone" to do all the final adjustments to the heights and so on and finally to get your measuring wheel and trudge round measuring the courses whilst from the stands come the usual remarks such as "Where's your other wheel, Guv'nor?"

The main course you have just built is for a very large first prize sponsored by a big Company, and in its design you have tried to incorporate certain problems that you feel are befitting the nature of the competition.

The afternoon has turned to evening, you are now drying out from your soaking, the course is finished and, after a final look round, you are feeling pretty pleased with yourself when a voice behind you says, "What's this supposed to be then?"—obviously referring to one of the fences. It is one of the competitors who has come for a preliminary look around to see what's in store for them on the morrow.

You refrain from any obvious reply, enquire after their health and wish them luck, and proceed to make your way back to your hotel, where you practically fall asleep in the bath and make plans for an early night.

But it is not to be, for a well-meaning friend has other ideas for you and calls you up just as you are about to retire and insists on collecting you and "showing you the town", which lasts until about one in the morning—so there goes your early night.

The first day of the show dawns bright and sunny, and you arrive at the showground and are greeted by the sight of two of your best looking fences seeming as if they had been hit by a bomb. After various enquiries you find that a very well-meaning Steward had thought they might have been in the way of a show class, and had moved them, hope you didn't mind, old chap. Of course you don't mind, nothing delights you more than having to do your work over again.

The time has now arrived to meet the Arena Party, which is a very smart military one, and a little time has to be spent explaining their various duties to them with regard to re-erecting the fences after being knocked down, keeping out of the way of the horses and so on, and also the rather tricky problem that at a show it will not be possible for the orders to be transmitted down the line of N.C.O.s, but as speed is so essential, they will have to take their orders direct from you.

Before the competition starts, the competitors have the opportunity of inspecting the course in order to enable them to make their own particular plans for dealing with fences and problems you have set them. This is certainly no time for the course builder to relax as he has to be on the alert for the character who would like to wedge the gate more firmly on its fittings, the one who would like the brush fence pulled farther out from the Oxer, and, of course, there are always the very "interesting" remarks to be heard regarding the distances you have set in the Doubles and Combination fences.

Obviously you can never be right for everyone, so you must always endeavour to set your fences and distances fairly, with the object of producing good jumping always in mind.

The competitors have now left the ring, and just before the competition starts one of the Judges might enquire how many clear rounds you expect to get; this is a fatal question, because if you answer that you expect about seven, it is an absolute certainty that you will get about twenty.

It is, however, your 'lucky day' today as the jumping is fine and produces about six clear rounds which go forward to make a very exciting jump-off, and your day is made when, as the winner goes round on his lap of honour after having collected his £200, he calls to you, "That was quite a nice course, John."

The centre fences are now removed quickly for the display, and as soon as this is done, you send the Arena Party off to a meal, impressing on them the time to be back so that the course can be re-set for the next class.

The display makes its dramatic exit and all is ready to re-erect the fences, but you only have three members of your party available; the others having met with difficulties in the meal tent and they arrive back, full of apologies, just as you and your three exhausted men have finished.

The last class is an exciting speed competition, and with the aid of the expert commentator, who whips the spectators into a state of extreme excitement, it provides a wonderful finish to a grand first day of the show.

You now have to break the news to your Party that the next day's course will now be built, but like the good chaps they are they realise that the sooner we start and get on with it, the less dates will be broken that evening; so as the Judges and Officials leave the Ring on their way to some well-earned refreshment, it's coats off and down to work.

One of the Officials, who is a bit behind the rest of the party, expresses his sympathy with you for having to work on and would you like a helping hand.

One day I will say, "Yes, please," and see what happens.

The final day of this great show arrives, and the competitors are walking the course for the final big competition when one of the Judges approaches you and enquires as to whether you are happy about the course being of sufficient severity so as not to get too many clears, because he feels it would spoil the class, and anyway he has a long way to go and would rather get home that evening, if possible; you hasten to assure him that you think all will be well.

By this time your luck has deserted you, in spite of your carefully planned course, the going is perfect, the competitors and their horses are on top form, the distances must be about right. You end up with the nice round figure of twenty clear rounds, and there ends the very nice friendship with your Judge.

After having thanked the Area Party for the wonderful way they carried out their rather exacting task, you see that the fences are organised for collection, if necessary, and retire to the Stewards' Room for a little liquid refreshment, and perhaps have the opportunity of meeting and thanking the Officials who have co-operated with you in such a helpful manner.

Except at shows close to home, you usually have to spend that night in the hotel, and there one often sits and reflects on the courses and the jumping over the past three days, and in spite of all the good-natured leg pulling of the competitors and the various little things that haven't gone exactly to plan, you have the feeling that everyone has rather enjoyed the show.

Your courses have given them enough to think about without being too tricky or too big in height, the problems you have set have been dealt with successfully by the majority and the winners have been very worthy ones.

Naturally your efforts do not always work out right—the weather, for example, can play a great part in affecting the jumping, especially if a heavy rainstorm comes when the competition is in progress, as apart from making the ground bad it can make your easy distances into very difficult ones.

Sometimes the ground doesn't jump as you anticipate it will; occasionally a ground that looks very lush and springy will jump very "dead", and vice versa, and, however carefully you weigh up the facts when designing the course and setting the distances, these conditions can upset your calculations, and you must alter the plan of campaign when dealing with the courses on the next day.

A problem which sometimes confronts a course builder is the lack of material available for his or her use; the only thing to do in this case is to try to obtain additional material such as straw bales or faggots to supplement the material already there.

However good a set of fences may be, a selection of fir tops or shrubs placed as decoration at the sides of the obstacles do much to increase the solidity of the fence and make them more attractive to look at from the spectators' point of view.

Your next show is some 250 miles away, so you might as well spend the rest of the evening starting to formulate a plan for that show, especially as we have a display by the Loamshire Cavalry, who would very much like the whole of the ring cleared for them; but before we start, let's have a good steak to get a bit of our strength back.

On a more serious note, in spite of all the hazards, the soakings and the hundred and one other things that can go wrong, there can be few things more satisfying to the course builder than seeing horse and rider jumping with ease and grace over one of his courses and providing the Public with such a wonderful spectacle.

No course builder must ever forget the importance of the novice horse and pony; they must always have the same thought and consideration when designing a course as one gives to those for the more experienced horses and ponies, and without the novices and the youngsters we would soon be without top-line jumpers; and if that ever happened, we wouldn't need any course builder, and I, personally, would hate that to happen as I like all the leg-pulling, the soakings, and am even beginning to like cold ham and chicken.

THE MATTER OF FORM

There is a tendency now to dress anyhow. But those who are not carefully dressed do not give the impression that they are capable of looking after a valuable—or indeed any pony. I have never known any of these oddly dressed folk to be first-class riders. The good horseman is invariably suitably dressed, there is something about him, even if his coat is threadbare, that bears witness to the fact that he is accustomed to the society of that great gentleman, the horse. There is no room for eccentricity in riding clothes, for there is a reason for every item of the horseman's attire.

Golden Gorse THE YOUNG RIDER

The Pony Club

COL. THE HON. C. GUY CUBITT, D.S.O., T.D.

LET US SUPPOSE, for a moment, that the reader is very young; or perhaps a parent anxious to do the right thing by his importunate offspring. The answer, in both cases, is the Pony Club, which has its headquarters at 16, Bedford Square, London, W.C.1.

Since its foundation in 1929 the Pony Club of Great Britain has gone from strength to strength. From small beginnings, it has grown up into an organisation of 60,000 members, with 250 units up and down the country.

It should hardly be necessary here to explain the aims of the Pony Club in detail. Let us just say that it exists to encourage young riders, and to enable them to develop the art of horsemanship in all its various aspects; and that, in order to join, it is not necessary for a child to own a pony.

Naturally, possession of a pony is a desirable asset. But, although the Pony Club is not in a position to provide ponies for its members to ride, there is nothing to stop children from hiring ponies from riding schools and using them to take part in the activities of the Club. In fact, many members do just this.

The numerous branches are self-contained, self-governing and self-supporting; and each has a District Commissioner, whose duty it is to appoint other officers of the branch and to see that the rules, which are anything but irksome, are properly observed. Large-scale operations, such as the Inter-Branch Championships for Horse Trials, Polo and Mounted Games, are organised from the Central Committee on a national basis; as indeed are the various conferences and Instructors' Courses, and the production of literature and films.

But it is the District Commissioners who arrange what are known as the

The Pony Club

Working Rallies, and it is these rallies that are the real backbone of the movement. They are designed to be both instructive and pleasurable, and they include instruction in stable management. It is expected that all members of the branch will take part in the rallies whenever possible, for it is upon the effective and successful organisation of these get-togethers that a branch either sinks or swims.

Of course, the young rider will learn nothing unless he (or she, for that matter) is interested in what is going on and can appreciate the necessity for basic instruction. And he is not likely to attend rallies unless he can be sure of enjoying them. The good Instructor—and the Club is interested in no other kind—knows all this. And he knows, too, that it is part of his job to see that his young charges derive the maximum benefit and satisfaction from such activities.

At a well-organised Working Rally one would expect to see riders, ponies and horses of various ages, sizes and capabilities. I suppose one might say that there is an equivalent in the class-room. The good teacher knows that if he concentrates on his brighter pupils and leaves the others to look after themselves, he is not doing his job properly. So it is with the Pony Club. If the Instructor is bored, so will his pupils be. Variety is essential in all things where the young are concerned. They will not tolerate interminable lecturing. As soon as their attention begins to wander—and preferably before this—they should be given the opportunity to do something themselves, whether it is the jumping that they are always itching to engage in, the mounted games that test a horse's obedience and the capacity of his rider to enforce discipline without resorting to rough-shod methods, or the kind of games in which the weaker members can participate without feeling that they are making fools of themselves.

Finally, the Instructor needs to ensure that both riders and ponies are in a fit condition to undertake the journey home. If he omits to do this, he is likely to have some very ferocious parents on his tail; and everyone knows how formidable the Pony Club mum can be! He may also have some irate riding-school proprietors to deal with. And he will deserve all he gets.

Most branches of the Pony Club hold an Annual Camp. Whether these are held in the ancestral homes of England—and they frequently are—or, as sometimes occurs, on racecourses and showgrounds, under canvas with the ponies on horse lines, the result should be the same, a happy atmosphere and plenty of opportunity for the campers to get to know each other at close quarters.

At these camps there are even jobs for the unfortunates who have no ponies to ride. They can help in the kitchens, in the horse lines and in the riding paddocks; and their contribution to the success of the camp is no small one.

On the holiday trail in the Highlands of Scotl

Now! Which is which?

Sacked!

The Pony Club

Even under the worst conditions of an English summer—and we all know what they can be—it is possible for any right-minded youngster to enjoy himself. After a very wet camp in 1962, a Pony Club mum was prompted to write in the following terms:

"Mary adored the whole week. The only dry thing that she brought home was her face sponge."

Perhaps I ought to add, after this, that it is normal Pony Club practice to insist on cleanliness as a primary part of the horseman's training, and that little Mary must somehow have managed to escape the vigilance of her guardians. Some children take this part of the instruction so literally that, on one occasion, a small boy was observed cleaning his pony's teeth with his own tooth brush!

There are many other forms of activity besides the Working Rally and the Annual Camp, such as visits to kennels and stud farms; mounted paper-chases, mock hunts, horse shows, hunter trials, special Pony Club Meets of Hounds, and expeditions of various kinds. The keynote is unobtrusive instruction. Learning without tears, in fact.

What about incentives? Well, there are these as well, of course. Efficiency Certificates are awarded in several categories dealing with riding and stable management. The keen eight- or nine-year-old has his chance to gain the modest "D" Certificate. "B" and "C" Certificates are within the reach of the average fourteen- and fifteen-year-olds who can ride and look after a reasonably well-mannered hunter; while the "A" Certificate, a much-coveted award held in high regard throughout the world, is reserved for those who obtain the highest standards. This demands the ability to adjust technique to embrace the more complicated arts of training a young horse on the flat, show jumping and galloping. Beyond this, there is an Honours award, for those who have the ability and determination to work for it.

Hunting Certificates are in three grades, ranging from an average standard to an advanced one. And, for the chosen few, there are what I might describe as the 1st XI events, the Horse Trials Championship, the Mounted Games Championship (which culminates at the "Horse of the Year" Show at Wembley in October) and the Polo Tournament. Let us take them in order.

The Horse Trials, as in the senior events, comprise a dressage test, a cross-country ride, and an elementary show-jumping phase; and the climax is reached when the winning teams and the winning individuals from 16 areas meet in the Team and Individual Championships. This is the supreme test of riding ability on an obedient and well-schooled animal.

The Mounted Games are strictly for teams, and are intended to encourage the keen and active member on a workaday pony. The games played in this competition are all of the kind that can be tried out at the Working Rallies, and are designed to quicken the riders' reactions and instil confidence. Even in the rough-and-tumble of such games as sack races, musical chairs or bending races, the carefully-trained pony will almost invariably come out on top. And this is how it should be.

The Polo Tournament is, as yet, confined to the few branches which have overcome the difficulty of finding suitable grounds on which to play. In the three years that this tournament has been going, it has been immensely successful, and the standard of play has improved out of all knowledge.

Perhaps it is as well to finish up with some practical considerations, and to emphasise that it was never the intention that the Pony Club should be the exclusive prerogative of the well-to-do. The entry fee is a mere 2s. 6d. for each member, and the annual subscription no more than 15s. Nor is it necessary for the young rider to dress extravagantly. If his clothes are well made, clean and subjected to proper brushing, it doesn't matter a jot how ancient they are. For the sake of safety, however, the rules do demand that all members wear a reinforced riding hat or cap when mounted. The Pony Club Badge, which members are asked to wear on all occasions when meeting together, costs 2s. A saddle—the most expensive single item of equipment—marked on the stirrup bar "Pony Club Approved", can be had from all saddlers at a basic cost of £20.

There is, of course, rather more to it than this brief summary suggests. But it is not my business to paraphrase the Pony Club Year Book, which gives a very full picture of the Club's activities in its 170 pages and is issued annually by Headquarters a the price of 3s. 6d. For anybody who wishes to know more about the affairs of the Pony Club, this is the book to get.

In the Pony Club of Great Britain the children from homes where there is little or no talk of horses can enjoy the companionship of kindred spirits, and learn to appreciate the love of horses and riding that is an integral part of the British character. And there is no colour bar, nor any form of racial or religious discrimination.

Foxhunting in the Welfare State

DORIAN WILLIAMS, M.F.H.

THE FUTURE might well call this the age of anachronisms. Our preoccupation with tradition even in an age of relentless progress enables us to retain with the minimum of embarrassment such splendidly archaic delights as beefeaters, bowler hats, tiaras and foxhunting. They are delightful and completely legitimate anachronisms showing as they do that as a nation we are not slavishly subservient to logic, that our own feet still being firmly on the ground—and our umbrella in the rack—progress will never be allowed to get completely out of hand.

Out of hand! But the cynic will say that nothing could be more out of hand in this day and age of intensified agriculture than a horde of people galloping madly over other people's land. Is not this, they will ask, carrying the preservation of feudal tradition too far?

During the first two centuries of foxhunting, the eighteenth and nineteenth centuries, the land was for the most part owned by the great feudal landlords; agriculture was in such poor shape that tenants were in no position to complain to the landlord of damage done to a farm by the hunt of which the landlord was invariably a leading member, if not the Master himself. In addition much more of the countryside was covered with woodlands and therefore the amount of hunting in open country was far less than today. It was, in fact, the open nature of the countryside in Leicestershire and Northamptonshire—"the Shires"—that made those midland counties the Mecca of foxhunting. Here, obviously, it was more *fun* than on the moors in the north or in the forests in the south. In addition, thanks to the agricultural revolution sparked off by Robert Bakewell, himself a midlander, the division of land and enclosures resulted in the jumping of fences, and the excitement, danger and hazards which jumping entailed, bringing a new pleasure to the chase. And pleasure it certainly was; for in the eighteenth and nineteenth centuries there was no such thing as barbed wire or excavated ditches to make fences unjumpable; there were few main roads and no petrol-eking traffic; no railways or canals. One could ride straight. Indeed on a good scenting day a hunt was like a race. Hence the cachet "riding to hounds" came to mean something as thrilling as nature could provide.

Such indeed was the pleasure inherent in foxhunting a hundred years ago that it became the most fashionable of all countryside pursuits; few people would dare to live in the country and not to hunt; many who lived in towns would feel it incumbent upon them to have a hunting "lodge" or "box" in the country in order that they could keep properly in the social swim; for England then was still governed by the foxhunting squires and the great feudal landlords.

These now legendary figures rated hunting as a priority in their lives. They kept magnificent establishments which cost them many thousands of pounds a year, but which also brought tremendous employment to the poverty-stricken countryside. They hunted huge tracts of lands. The Duke of Beaufort for instance hunted the country which stretched from Bristol to Banbury; the Earl of Berkeley, though his kennels were at Berkeley Castle on the Severn, hunted as far east as Marble Arch; the Duke of Grafton kennelled his hounds in Surrey but hunted in Suffolk and Northamptonshire (in the 1740s he introduced an Act of Parliament which resulted in the building of Westminster Bridge, so that his hounds might cross the Thames more easily!); Earl Fitzwilliam hunted in Yorkshire and the Midlands.

The stamina, the pure physical toughness of these great, allegedly port-drinking squires is beyond belief. To read today their hunting diaries, telling of 60 mile journeys in ill-sprung equipages on appalling roads, of 12 hours in the saddle, followed by gargantuan, four-hour-long repasts, is to make one feel that we in our age are pygmies by comparison.

In the middle of the nineteenth century, due to rising costs resulting from the industrial revolution and the Napoleonic Wars, many of the great aristocratic Masters of hounds felt unable to continue, and so it was that subscription packs were started. Often his lordship remained as Master and this led to awkward and embarrassing situations. The hounds were *his*; much of the country was *his*; but the subscribers who were paying for the upkeep of the establishment felt that they were entitled to a say in the administration. This his lordship bitterly resented, and so the history of foxhunting in the nineteenth century is full of rows and rumpuses, and the formation of many new packs which were largely independent of the feudal influence.

Foxhunting in the Welfare State

By the twentieth century the picture of foxhunting as we know it today had become more or less established. There were, speaking rather generally, four types of packs. There were firstly the great family packs which were centred on the ancestral home, where also were the kennels: Badminton, the Duke of Beaufort; Brocklesby, the Earl of Yarborough; Belvoir Castle, the Duke of Rutland; Berkeley Castle, the Earl of Berkeley; Bowhill, the Duke of Buccleuch; Alnwick, the Duke of Northumberland; Milton, the Earl Fitzwilliam; Wynnstay, Sir Watkin Williams Wynn; and others. These establishments were magnificently maintained, and although they were in every case subscription packs, the contribution of the Master himself was so much greater than everyone else's that his sway was virtually absolute. The subscriber contributed to the cost, but had little or no control over the administration, the hounds, kennels and everything connected with the hunt belonging to his Grace, or his lordship.

Visitors to these near-private hunts were seldom *persona grata*. Badminton or Alnwick, or whichever it was, was the centre of a neighbourhood, and it was for this neighbourhood that sport was being provided. Strangers were not encouraged, and for the most part, their financial assistance was not needed.

The second section consisted of the famous "Shires". In contrast to the family packs these hunts, based for the most part in Leicestershire, depended almost entirely on the support of visitors. Insufficiently populated, there were not enough wealthy people to keep a hunt going. The result was that whereas a family pack had been in the same hands, from father to son, for centuries, the "Shires" had constant changes of Mastership. A wealthy Master would take over for perhaps ten or twelve seasons, spend a fortune, and then give way to someone else prepared to do the same; but such was the sport in this foxhunters' paradise that people flocked from all over the country, indeed all over the world, for a season's hunting. It was the subscription of these visitors alone that kept the hunt going. As a rule when referring to the "Shires" one is referring to the Quorn, the Cottesmore, the Belvoir, the Pytchley, the Fernie.

The third section has always been called "the provinces", and as the name suggests the provinces are really "the Shires'" poor relation. Possessing splendid but not quite so splendid hunting country as the Shires they neither attracted the type of Master nor the number of visitors that the Shires did. Being also sparsely populated they were to a certain extent dependent upon outsiders, but not so much as the Shires, and indeed they were often inaccessible. On the other hand it was not necessary to keep up so lavish an establishment, and so in the provinces there is a history of longer masterships and therefore greater stability. The Arkwrights with the Oakley, the Brasseys with the Heythrop, the Barclays with the Puckeridge, successive Lord

Foxhunting in the Welfare State

Willoughby de Brokes with the Warwickshire, Selby Lowndes with the Whaddon Chase, Lord Hillingdon with the Grafton, Hogwood Lonsdale with the Bicester: these are a few examples of long tenancies with the provincial packs.

Finally there was the type of pack that is neither family, nor Shires, nor Provinces. Perhaps 50 per cent of the packs of hounds in England at the beginning of the twentieth century could be included in this fourth category. That they were not in one of the others is solely for geographical reasons. Either they were not part of a great estate or else they were in a part of the country less well suited to foxhunting than the midlands; bounded on one side by the sea perhaps, fenland, moors, downs, sparsely wooded or over-wooded, suburban. The sport they provided was often of the highest order, but their territory was less fashionable.

Surprisingly, despite two world wars, a social revolution and the development of nuclear energy, the overall picture has changed remarkably little in sixty years. There are still Beauforts and Buccleuchs, Northumberlands and Fitzwilliams, Bathursts and Burghleys who maintain family packs though run on a very much less regal scale than hitherto. There is still the Quorn and the Cottesmore, the Belvoir and the Pytchley, the first two in particular with visitors flocking up each week to a Quorn Monday or Cottesmore Tuesday.

There is still the more personal atmosphere of the Warwickshire, the Grafton and the Bicester, with their smaller fields and greater stability. There are still well over a hundred hunts in the great outer perimeter from Wales and the West to the eastern seaboard; from the Fells and the Dales to the highlands; and Yorkshire, perhaps the greatest hunting centre of all.

Despite these divisions all hunts today have common problems, and most of them have found the same solutions. Costs have risen enormously, so that a pack of hounds today costs at least £2500 a year for each day of the week hunted. In other words a two day a week pack will cost £5000 a year to run: a four day a week pack will cost £10,000. So subscriptions are raised and every kind of money-making venture is resorted to: dances, whist-drives, pools, sweepstakes, jumble sales.

Farming today is practised more seriously, and so most hunts employ a full time secretary to deal with the farmers' problems and complaints where they affect the hunt. Farmers are encouraged to hunt, for nothing of course, and their children invited to join the Pony Club.

Most hunts have supporters' clubs that help both in raising funds and spreading goodwill.

Yet though the problems and their solutions are common, though the purpose of the sport is identical, the hunting of the fox through the medium of hounds and the pleasure that accrues in the studying of this art of venery,

Foxhunting in the Welfare State

the joy of following hounds mounted on a horse; yet it cannot be denied that great contrasts exist in the different hunts, and a newcomer to the sport, or to the country, would have to make up his mind whether *his* idea of the sport of foxhunting lay with such as the Duke of Beaufort's or the newly formed Banwen. Between the two there exists a considerable gulf, though, in fact, the differences are but matters of degree.

To give some idea of these contrasts and differences it might be helpful to set out a few hunts from each category with their individual characteristics and requirements; and if these, perhaps, are a little light hearted and exaggerated, may I, as a Master of Hounds myself, be forgiven!

THE FAMILY PACKS

The Duke of Beaufort's. This hunt, without argument is *the* hunt, though except for the sport it is as untypical of hunting as it could possibly be. The hunt staff wear *green*, the family livery; members of the hunt wear *blue* coats with buff collar and facings. Unless obviously a visiting master, wearing a velvet cap, one feels a little out of things hunting in scarlet, though this can be mitigated by referring to the Duke as "Master" in a very familiar manner, or, if really daring, as "Hugh". It is a little awe-inspiring to hunt at Badminton—and expensive (just how expensive is a secret between you and the Secretary); but it is a great experience, as you would expect with one whose car number is, rightly, M.F.H. 1.

The Burghley. A complete contrast, Lord Exeter's private pack, re-formed only five years ago. No subscription, delightfully informal, it all takes you back to the start of hunting 250 years ago. Lord Exeter and staff wear green; everyone else anything they like.

The Buccleuch. The Beaufort of the North. £40 a horse, which means, more or less, if you hunt one day a week; genuine people, few visitors, glorious country.

THE SHIRES

The Quorn. Masters: Mrs. Murray Smith and can't remember, because of frequent recent changes. Subscription—another secret, but it will cost you £100 a season at least, and up to £10 a day if you go out on a Monday. Wonderful pack of hounds, wonderful country, terrifying crowd, especially on Mondays.

The Belvoir. Four Masters, but all sportsmen even if it is like a committee. A pure bred English pack, all black and tan in colour, which is rare these days. Subscription for man and wife, hunting two days, is round about £150. £5

Foxhunting in the Welfare State

a day cap for strangers. The Leicestershire side is as good as the Quorn; Lincolnshire side less smart, very genuine.

The Cottesmore. Centres round "character" Major "Bob" Hoare, huntsman and joint Master; seldom seen without smile, therefore very welcoming. Everything goes like hell. Just about as smart as Quorn, and a little more personal. Worth living there as it only costs you £40 p.a. £100 if you don't. £5 cap. Most of the great names in hunting history have been Masters at one time or another.

THE PROVINCES

The Warwickshire. Smart black collar to the coat. Just about smartest hunt of "the provinces". Lovely country spoilt a bit by Birmingham. £40 a day. A bit frightening at first, but very friendly beneath surface, as few visitors. Despite their difficulties still a "prestige" pack.

The Whaddon Chase. Famous for rows—until 10 years ago! (Author became Master in 1954.) Once called London's Leicestershire because mostly grass. Very smart and fashionable between wars. Now ordinary, and *fun*; but big fields and big subscription, over £100 unless you're resident, which most people aren't.

The Grafton. Potentially most ideal hunting country in midlands, but short of money. Colonel Neil Foster senior Master; nothing like as frightening as people think. Small, happy field; good hounds. Subscription £80. Worth it. (Author was Master of Grafton 1951–54!)

The Atherstone. Hunt with great tradition and white collar, grey facings to evening red coats. A little Birminghamised now. £45 subscription; very reasonable. Colonel Morrison is the hound expert, anti the "establishment"; good fun and connoisseur of wine. Happy.

The Heythrop. Heart of "the establishment". No. 1 prestige pack. No fault of Captain Ronnie Wallace, perhaps greatest living huntsman, amateur or professional, today. Hunt staff in green coats reminding of Beaufort connection. Huge fields but glorious open country. Sport virtually guaranteed. Subscription (?). No visitors. Great social advantages if you can say you hunt with Heythrop, or better still "with Ronnie".

THE FOURTH CATEGORY

The Zetland. Black collar for members of Old Raby Hunt Club(!). £40 per horse. More plough than there used to be, but genuine hunting country,

I freely admit that the best of my fun I owe it to horse and hound
G. J. Whyte Melville

Dorian Williams, Master of the Whaddon Chase, leading the field near Beachampton

Moving off from Badminton House: the Duke of Beaufort with his hounds

Foxhunting in the Welfare State

typical of Yorkshire hunts. Master, Colin MacAndrew, on fringe of "establishment"; very popular, problems surmounted with charm.

The Puckeridge—or Barclayshire—Barclays having been in charge all but 70 years. Subscription only £30 a day or £2 cap. Very reasonable. Plough; not much jumping, but real hound-work. Undemanding people. Unfrightening.

The Blackmore Vale. Subscription only £25 per horse; dark blue plush waistcoat with evening wear—but take no notice of that. Probably the "shire" of the West. Lot of retired generals. Master, Count de Pelet; foreign sounding, but English type. All pretty happy, still visited a little by shade of Miss Guest, Master since 1914, died 1962.

The Golden Valley. What a glorious name, for ideal country! Subscription £10! Small fields, no problem, few visitors, mostly farmers. This healthy happy state due to Masters, wealthy Mrs. Guest, knowledgeable Mr. Bishop. Suggest a house is bought there without further ado.

The Torrington Farmers. Subscription £5 5s. Typical of the many small packs all over the country that show tremendous sport in unfashionable country for unfashionable fields. Mostly farmers, welcome everywhere, accent on fun; the whole thing summed up in genial Frank Heal, Founder, Master, Huntsman, presiding spirit for 25 years. Hunting at its most genuine.

The Banwen. (The new Miners' pack in South Wales.) Subscription 2s. 6d. per day. Dress optional. Object of the exercise to catch foxes, otherwise uncatchable and making nuisance of themselves. Achievement: the scotching, once and for all, of the illusion that hunting is the sport and pastime of none other than the idle rich; cruel and un-necessary at that.

Take your pick. It can be smart and expensive, or 2s. 6d. a day; but whichever end of the scale is chosen there will, without a shadow of a doubt, be sport, companionship, exercise, and *fun*.

HUNTING AS IT APPEARS TO MR. JORROCKS
"'Unting fills my thoughts by day, and many a good run I have in my sleep. Many a dig in the ribs I gives Mrs. J. when I think they are running into the warmint (renewed cheers). No man is fit to be called a sportsman wot doesn't kick his wife out of bed on a haverage once in three weeks."

R. S. SURTEES

Jockeyship

LIEUT.-COLONEL TOM NICKALLS

MEN HAVE RACED horses since they first tamed and broke the wild horse to carry them. Styles of riding have evolved since earliest times, but when the first saddle was put on a horse's back it must have caused revolutionary rethinking in terms of riding for speed.

It has been recently written that the introduction of the stirrup iron in early mediaeval times caused almost as much tactical change in battle as the invention of gunpowder. For the horseman, so equipped, had a seat so much stronger, and leverage on his lance so greatly superior to his stirrup-less adversary as to make him the certain winner in combat.

There can be little doubt that the stirrup had an equally far-reaching effect on the style of race-riding.

However, from the impressions given us by horse artists since the late seventeenth century there seems to have been little change of style in race-riding since the sport started on an organised basis in the time of Charles II (Royal Ascot was started only about forty years after the Restoration) until the arrival of the "American seat" in this country at the turn of the last century—of which, more anon.

But just how do jockeys make horses go? The more one studies this absorbing question (to most of us who ride, or, even, who bet on racing) the more difficult it becomes to say exactly why, and how, the methods employed do in fact make the horse "put his best foot forward".

Ask almost any steeplechase jockey who has ridden on the flat which of the two forms of racing demand the most skill, and he will answer "Steeplechasing".

That bold and brilliant jump jockey, Jack Dowdeswell, once said, "Flat racing? It's a piece of cake! All you have to do is to canter your horse down to the start, and bring him back as fast as you know how!" And Jack, Champion National Hunt Jockey of 1946–47, was a pretty good performer under the other code. As indeed is "Davy" Jones, who rode a Cheltenham

Jockeyship

Gold Cup Winner (Red Rower) before he really made his name under Jockey Club Rules.

A slight over simplification no doubt—as any flat race jockey would instantly claim!

Though flat race jockeys have no experience of the skilful presentation of a horse at sixteen or twenty fences, and sitting tight when the partnership is under strain, nevertheless most flat race jockeys would outride the average steeplechase jockey in a set-to from the last fence to the winning post. And though the flat race rider has not the same problems with regard to fences, he can justly claim that everything happens so much quicker in flat racing that a jockey requires a higher degree of skill, in co-ordinating his conscious to his reflex actions.

To seize the sometimes fleeting opportunities presented in a flat race, a jockey has to make split second decisions, and it must become second nature to him to anticipate events.

But when we have said all that, we have only scraped the edge of the problem of riding on the flat. For matters of tactics can be learnt with experience—but what is the mystique which some brilliant jockeys seem to possess of infusing their mounts not only with the will to win but with the ability to do so?

Watch a field of apprentice riders on board racehorses that are "easy" rides, and all of whom one has seen racing well and consistently for experienced jockeys. Somehow the horses seldom seem to be racing as they would for jockeys. They get spread out over half a furlong—they gallop unbalanced, and idly, despite a volume of energy on the part of their small riders which one would think worthy of better results. And to show that some of them (the horses) are not doing their best, "form" is often turned upside down.

One could be pardoned for thinking that the racing seat practised by our remoter grandparents must surely be more effective than the cramped, tucked-up, crouching "seat" now practised—and furthermore, that a man, well able to use his legs, sitting down in the saddle and driving his horse so to speak in front of him, as old-timers used to do, would get more out of the animal. But strangely it is not so, as an American jockey named Tod Sloan was the first to discover. As a matter of fact, I believe he got the idea from negro boys who used to ride that way in the States. However that may be, it was he who first practised the style in this country towards the close of the 'nineties, and in so doing caused a complete revolution in the manner of race riding.

It is difficult not to suppose that Tod Sloan's immediate and astonishing success in this country was as much accounted for by his novel race riding tactics as his method of actually riding his mounts.

Jockeyship

Hitherto, it had been the practice to race at a very steady half speed for the first half or three-quarters of a race, and then to finish at best pace with a terrific flourish. Naturally such a method of race riding would suit neither the sharp American race tracks, with their small oval circuits, nor the exaggerated forward style of riding, for Tod Sloan practically lay along his horses' necks, and gave them no assistance at all with his legs.

Anyway, Mr. Sloan carried all before him, and, to the amazement, and I have no doubt the intense irritation, of the English jockeys, showed them that the way to win races was to run them "all the way". Naturally, when they all started to copy his methods and tactics, his successes were not so overwhelming, but some idea of the way that this new style of riding caught on can be gauged from the following remarks and figures I found the other day in the racing papers of that experienced and successful owner Mr. Walter Raphael, who bred and owned such classic winners as Tagalie, the last filly to win the Epsom Derby, Louviers (Two Thousand Guineas) and Bettina (One Thousand Guineas). "In this year (1900) there were several American jockeys riding here. It has so often been debated whether their monkey crouch seat in the saddle gave them an advantage or not over the English jockeys, that I think it advisable, without giving any opinion myself, to give a few statistics, which, to say the least of it, gives one *furieusement à penser*.

		Mounts	Wins	Winning Percentage	
L. REIFF	American	553	143	25·85	(2)
S. LOATES	English	672	137	16·93	
J. REIFF	American	604	124	20·52	(4)
C. MADDEN	English	662	96	14·59	
J. RICKABY	English	476	84	17·64	
TOD SLOAN	American	310	82	26·45	(1)
M. CANNON	English	490	82	16·73	
B. RIGBY	American	447	68	15·21	
J. H. MARTIN	American	326	52	15·95	
W. HALSEY	English	205	40	19·51	
D. MAHER	American	128	27	21·09	(3)

Here you have 11 jockeys, five English and six American, and the first four places (by average) are held by Americans with very fine averages."

This reads oddly similar to the wave of success currently attending the Australian jockeys riding in this country!

Tod Sloan's style was not slavishly copied. It would have been impossible for the senior jockeys, so thoroughly grounded in the old style, to adopt so

Epsom, with the field rounding Tattenham Corner

Petite Etoile with Lester Piggott in the saddle—a veritable flyer, ridden by one of the leading contemporary jockeys

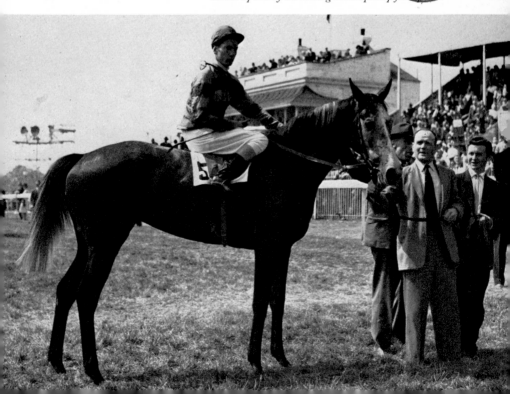

Jockeyship

exaggerated a "monkey crouch". So it was that a modified form of the American crouch was evolved, as the old-timers pulled up their leathers by half and learnt to ride a finish on their knees. This became the classic English style as we now know it, and despite the successes of the Australians, it has no superior on our racecourses, with their gradients, and long stretches of straight galloping, where a horse needs more help and more driving than on the flat American and Australian-type ovals.

In the U.S.A. they teach their racehorses to run "flat out" all the way—this they are obliged to do, owing to the frequent bends on their courses. Such tactics are considered rather unethical here, so that every now and again a bright jockey steals a race by dashing off with a long lead, and maintaining it. "Steve" Donoghue set rather a fashion of winning the Derby that way in the early 'twenties, but now, alas, they seem to have gone back to the business of waiting about and dawdling in long-distances races—the Derby nowadays being run at a very sober pace for the first half of the journey, compared with the Derbies of thirty and forty years ago.

Part of the trouble is probably due to the reluctance of trainers to see their horses in front, or to train them to race that way—and part to the inability of so many jockeys to judge pace accurately (except the Australians, and they dislike making the running).

An instance of the way in which some trainers might be surprised at the improvement their charges could make if allowed to race in front occurred, greatly to my amusement, some years ago. There was a horse, let us call him "A", running in a minor event at Nottingham, who had been second, or close up third, in his last four races. He seemed to have nothing much to beat, though there was another horse in the race, let us call him "C", who had shown a modicum of form, though I had formed the opinion that he was ungenerous. I fancied "A" very much to beat "C"—and to win. But when I got to the races I heard "over the grapevine" that "A" (who was said by his connections to be a thorough rogue) was "not off", his jockey having had a good bet on "C" who was to be ridden by a pal of his. As usually happens in such circumstances, "A" drifted out to a long price in the market, while "C" became a hot favourite. From the moment the tapes flew up the jockey on "A" sent his mount off as though all the devils in hell were after him. By the time he reached half way with five furlongs still to go he was leading by ten or twelve lengths.

The idea behind these tactics was simple enough: ride the horse into the ground, and he will stop to a walk in the home straight, but by the time they were into the last quarter of a mile "A"'s jockey was sitting still, with the horse going surprisingly strongly under him. With another half furlong gone, and still no sound of passing hooves, "A"'s jockey began looking round, and

he crucial moment at Goodwood

Jockeyship

what he saw brought no comfort to his soul. The jockey on "C" was hard at work and getting no response. As I had thought, "C" was anything but a battler and had been given far too much to do, in the certainty that "A" would come back to him. The result—a capital win for "A" at a long price with his rider still holding him hard by the head. Nor was he particularly pleased when I congratulated him on the original way in which he had ridden this winner!

How often indeed do we hear jockeys praised for riding a brilliant race when they have brought their mounts up on the inside, and sneaked through between the leader and the rails "to steal" the race in the last two strides. But with equal frequency, and no little heat, is the employer of such tactics reviled, when they fail to come off.

It is so much a matter of luck. An uninterrupted run on the outside of the field may not be so spectacular, but in nine cases out of ten is more likely to succeed than threading a passage through a closely packed field, and challenging between one or more horses.

Of course part of the skill of jockeyship lies in knowing what is going on around you in the race. A first class jockey will know how his rivals are going —and therefore which horses are the ones to follow, or which he has to beat. He will, too, have a shrewd idea before the race starts which of his rivals are likely to be the most dangerous, and how they are likely to run their race.

A jockey who can tell a trainer after a race not only how his own horse ran but also how some of the others ran their races is of course a pearl of great price.

An experienced jockey of my acquaintance riding in a race at Yarmouth not so long ago noticed a young jockey having no end of a job to keep his horse from running too prominently. Returning to unsaddle he remarked how "strong" this other had been, to which the young jockey replied that he'd had orders not to show the colt up, as he was "well in" a Nursery at Newbury the following week, ending up with—"he must have won had I let him go".

It so happens that the young jockey could not ride the horse at Newbury owing to a prior claim on his services. But when telling the trainer so, he advised him to put my friend up, as he was the only jockey who had noticed what was afoot at Yarmouth! The colt fairly trotted up at Newbury with the experienced jockey on board.

There are some jockeys who became quite well known (to the "Regulars") through never riding winners. Many of the big stables have a fairly experienced jockey and workrider who gets up on the "unfancied" ones. It is desperately hard luck, but their mounts are always the young and inexperienced two year olds or the three year olds running weight off for handicaps, or the slow ones that the top class jockey, retained by the stable, doesn't deign to ride. Some of these fellows are very good horsemen with wonderful hands—they must have, to do some of the things that they are asked to do! But if they really ride well, they often get "a break" in the end, being taken up by other trainers to ride their fancied ones.

This whole business of non-triers is a very delicate affair. Naturally no one ever tells a jockey he is not to win—and no one expects to see their jockey fighting to check their horse in the closing stages of a race even if it is not meant to be "off". The jockey's orders will have been so worded as to leave him in no doubt that he is not to be placed, without ever saying so directly. While the expectation will be that any "controlling" will be done only in the race, well covered up amongst the other runners, so that there should be no question of the jockey being in the position envisaged in the concluding sentence of his orders, when for good form's sake, the trainer says, "Of course, win if you can, but don't be too hard on him."

A jockey knows just what to do, when the trainer says to him before putting him up—"Give him a nice race, he's not quite ready yet. I want him to enjoy himself, but I'd like your opinion of him—we think he may be quite useful—and there are some pretty smart ones in this field." In other words, he will be expected to measure strides with some of the smart ones for as long as he dare, without, however, getting so compromised that he has to ride a finish, or ease him out of the "shake up" coming to the distance, where everything can be seen.

A jockey's response to such orders as, "Don't overdo it—he's better in at Kempton next week", may well land him in trouble with the Stewards. So once again we see how necessary it is for a jockey to have brains! The explanation must be foolproof and not implicate the trainer—who is sure to be asked first, "Were you satisfied with the riding of your jockey?" It is considered bad form for the trainer to admit that he was not. Many punters think that the jockey should first be asked if he was satisfied with the orders he received from the trainer. One jockey who rode for a big stable always knew when his mount was not to be doing its level best. On the occasions when it was—and the stable had had "the lot on", his lordship used to stand by while the trainer put the jockey up and gave him his final instructions. But when it was a case of "Not today", he would drift away as the saddling bell rang, saying, "Well, I think I'll just go and see how they bet!" Once this routine became established there was no need for the trainer to give any orders!

Another part of the make-up of most jockeys is the Ready Excuse. One wonders how many fortunes have been lost as a result of remarks like, "Must have won it, but for carrying the winner for a hundred yards after turning

Jockeyship

into the straight", as the jockey unsaddles. Or, more frequently, when dismounting from one that has finished sixth or seventh, "I'd say we were third best, might even have troubled the winner if I'd given her a hard race."

I have said enough to give some idea of the many qualities a successful jockey needs to cultivate. How many of them, I often wonder, manage to suppress a smile when listening to long-winded instructions from trainers, and worse still, owners, as to the manner in which their horses are to be ridden. As one famous trainer is reputed to have said, "If my jockey has any intelligence he will know better than me how to ride the race. If he hasn't any intelligence, he is sure to forget everything he's been told as soon as he gets out on the course."

The other side of this particular problem seems a fitting conclusion to this essay. It concerns an irate jockey (attributed, variously and wrongly to Danny Maher, Frank Wootton, etc.) who rounded on a fat and pompous-looking owner who had upbraided him for riding a shocking race. "Who are you to accuse me of riding a bad race?" he wrathfully declared. "You've never ridden a race in your life." "No", came the reply, "and I've never laid an egg; but I've eaten a good few, and I reckon I know a good one from a bad!"

Steve Donoghue (1884–1945) rode in 14,008 races and won 1,844, the Derby six times, including a hat trick and the Queen Alexandra Stakes at Ascot on Brown Jack for six consecutive years.

Of all our relations with the dumb creation, there is none in which man has so entirely the best of it as the one-sided partnership that exists between the horse and his rider.

One white foot, buy a horse,
Two white feet, try a horse,
Three white feet, look well about him,
Four white feet, do without him.
OLD RHYME

The Equestrian Age of Reason

E. HARTLEY EDWARDS

IF OUR APPROACH to equitation is to be successful, we must above all things employ logical thinking in our dealings with the horse. Each step in his training must follow naturally and logically the preceding one. Nothing that we do, the pundits admonish us, must be contradictory in any way. Few would disagree with these dictums, certainly not I. Yet if we have reached what Benoist-Gironière terms the equestrian age of reason, I cannot understand—possibly because I attended a school which came well down the list in academic achievement in a recent public schools survey—why the age of reason takes such an unconscionable time to embrace the logical use of saddlery, unless it is that the majority of people who buy saddlery went to schools even lower down the list than mine.

After all, saddlery is the basis of our contact with the horse and the means by which we exert control over him, and we should all look rather silly making profound and undoubtedly reasonable observations on the art of equitation without having those means which would enable us to put them into practice.

As a saddler I see rather more of the commodity than most people, and perhaps more too of the illogicalities practised with the goods from which I make my livelihood.

My invariable custom is to start the day with a kind of C.O.'s inspection of workshops, and it was with these thoughts in mind that I commenced one of my recent eight o'clock tours.

Shop number one is a saddle shop where we make, amongst other types, a modern spring-tree saddle which we call an All Purpose or General Purpose Saddle (Fig. 5). Would that it had been christened by any other name! Its title was intended to imply that one could use it for hunting, jumping, cross country events and a certain amount of dressage. Today, if one is doing serious dressage, it would not be ideal because its design would tend to put the rider too far forward and somewhat in advance of the horse's movement and balance. Otherwise the design of the tree (Fig. 1) fulfils these purposes very satisfactorily.

The points and therefore the bars are advanced from the sloped head some three inches further forward than would be possible in the older type of conventional hunting saddle (see Fig. 2, Rigid tree), and so, in conjunction with the dipped sprung seat, position the rider in accordance with the basic principle of modern equitation that the weight should be carried as nearly as possible over the horse's point of balance (a line drawn through the withers

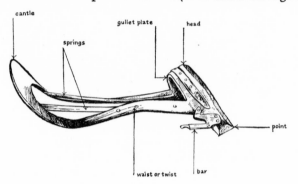

Figure 1 A spring-tree, showing the points

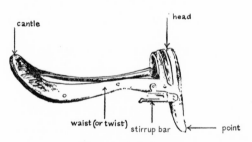

Figure 2 A rigid tree

to the ground when the horse is walking and moving forward as the speed increases) (Figs. 3 and 4). Even so a percentage of people who buy them expect to be able to indulge in all these activities, including dressage and riding in show classes without, in the latter case, the saddle covering up the (usually much exaggerated) shoulder of their horse. The impossibility of producing one saddle in which one can compete proficiently in all of these specialised branches of equitation I am prepared to explain patiently. I am not, however, prepared to explain, at least not without a certain amount of acerbity, why an All Purpose or General Purpose or any other saddle should fit every horse in the stable. You may have a general *fitting* tree which will fit the average back; but if you have a round cob and a spiney withered blood weed, one saddle can not possibly fit them both. To tell me that you once had a saddle that fitted everything—ponies, horses, the lot—is to invite a blistering reply. It is about as sensible and as true as saying that your grandfather, who stood 6' 4", once had a pair of trousers which fitted both him and your father (who was 5' 8" and 48" round the middle) and are now being worn by your twelve-year-old nephew. The truth is that you once

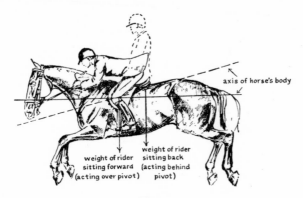

Figure 3

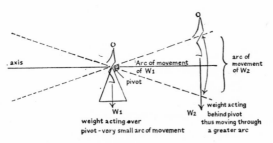

Figure 4

had a saddle which you put on every horse you ever owned, and if they all had much the same shape of back, you got away with it.

At least I am now largely spared the long and indecisive arguments with gentlemen (and ladies too) who until a few years ago determinedly resisted the advance of reason, about the merits of the modern saddle as opposed to the good old conventional saddle resolutely tipping the rider back well behind the movement, despite his attempts to be "with it". I can hear them now, "Ah! What happens if you land over a fence and your knees slip forward over those damned rolls? How d'you get back?" If your knees had gone that far forward on a modern saddle, where on earth would you be on a saddle without them? Surely clasping his ears or on the floor with no earthly chance of getting back. Spring trees too caused much derision, however patiently I explained that they gave the seat a resilience which it would be impossible to attain with the old-fashioned rigid trees. By being so resilient they "gave" as it were to the movement of the back, they enabled too the driving force of the rider's seat bones to be transmitted through the saddle to the horse instead of the effort being largely wasted when a rigid tree was used; and, of course, apart from giving more comfort to the horse they gave greater comfort to the rider. "Comfort" produced a snort of disgust, and usually these critics, having had their fun criticising something which they had never tried, moved off to their current year's motor car, switched the heater on and drove off. I always expected them to get into at least a 1904 De Dion Bouton or something of that ilk, but they never did!

There are very few of these redoubtable diehards left now—perhaps the age of reason engulfed them. In a funny way I rather miss them.

On the other side of the shop a batch of show saddles (Fig. 6) was being finished. The seats had got a slight dip to them, but the flaps were nearly cut straight in front so as to give the judge (as though he couldn't see) a clear view of the shoulder. Because the flaps are cut so straight it is necessary for the stirrup bars to be set back an inch or two more than usual, so that the leather shall lie down the centre of the flap and allow room for the rider's knee, incidentally encouraging the rider to sit as far back as he can. If the bars were placed in the ordinary way, the rider's knee would be off and in front of the flap. The panels were of very thin felt covered with leather, so that the saddle should fit close and not interfere with the line of the back. All were fitted with point straps, an additional girth strap coming beneath the point and allowing the saddle to remain a little further back than normal whilst permitting the girth to lie in its correct and usual place.

I admired the workmanship whilst secretly thinking what a pity it was to expend so much care and skill on a thing of such bad design.

Is the judge quite so stupid that all these little subterfuges should be necessary? After all, if he has any doubts as to the animal's conformation, they will always be resolved when he has the saddles removed.

There was another show saddle hanging up half made over the bench which had a label on denoting that it was a special order. This was a different cup of tea altogether. The seat was bigger and had a really good shape to it, the flap was cut much further forward than in the others, the bars were therefore in the usual place and the panel was not so thin, and instead of being of the Rugby pattern resembled the Saumur type (i.e. a panel incorporating a slight knee roll). As with the others, a point strap was fitted.

The Equestrian Age of Reason

I looked again at the first batch and mentally sympathised with the judges who were now doomed to sit in them. If giving the judge a good ride is half the battle, these would do little to help. One of them was little Miss So and So's, and whilst she might conceivably sit in it, or rather on it, it would certainly be a tight squeeze for most of the judges I knew, and one in particular being well over six feet tall was going to suffer agonies.

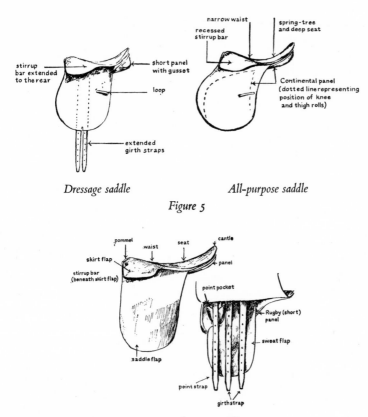

Dressage saddle   All-purpose saddle

Figure 5

Figure 6 Showing saddle

Why on earth not have a good practical saddle? By all means have the point strap on, for it is useful and does put both saddle and rider over the point of balance in the more collected paces and behind the shoulder muscle; but why insult the judge's intelligence by having a saddle which suggests that he will be taken in by its appearance on the horse's back, and then add injury to his person by making him ride in it?

The Equestrian Age of Reason

I passed on to Shop No. 2. Here is made horse-clothing, boots and various oddments which don't fit into any of the other shops.

Some sheepskin numnahs are ready to go to the despatch department; the skins are good and the wool close and springy, and they are all to fit either the All Purpose Saddles or one of the jumping saddles, as well as a few for children's saddles. Numnahs are my pet abomination. I spend years designing a saddle that will put the rider as close to the horse as possible, then I have to make numnahs for them which immediately puts the rider that much further away again. I know that there are certain horses which may go better wearing a numnah of this type, but these are very few compared with the number who wear them unnecessarily. In many cases numnahs are purchased for the not very good reason that the saddle does not fit without one, the obvious solution being to have the saddle properly regulated. Often the numnah, particularly when it reaches the inevitable state of resembling a dirty knotted mat, causes more harm than good, overheating the back and giving rise to galls and the like. Many are purchased for no better reason than that of "Keeping up with the Joneses"!

One machinist was at work binding some of the mesh anti-sweat rugs. These are a most practical type of horse clothing employing the same principle as the string vest. The mesh creates air pockets next to the body which are a form of insulation. By so doing they assist the horse to cool off without becoming chilled and discourage "breaking out" after hunting or racing. In the stable the rug insulates the body against excessive cold or heat. In order that the layer of insulating pockets can be formed it is necessary for the rug to be used under a top sheet. Without the latter it is of little value and yet how frequently are these rugs seen, particularly at race meetings, without a top covering, thereby nullifying their usefulness.

And so to Shops 3 and 4, both bridle shops and festooned with finished goods which only partially conceal the voluptuous charms of the hundred or more "pin-up lovelies" which decorate the walls. There are a group of show bridles, mostly for ponies. They are cut from the very light-weight butts which we keep specially for this type of bridle. I hope that the recipients of these very elegant little bridles will treat them with the respect they deserve and not expect them to stand up to the rigours endured by the heavier hunting bridle. So many people expect them to do both jobs, and then complain when the show bridle used for hunting and exercising as well does not stand up to its work.

Two or three of these bridles were exceptionally light with the reins only $\frac{3}{8}''$ wide. I appreciate that little hands have difficulty in encompassing two pairs of reins, but few people seem to realise that these reins with very little use begin to look and feel rather like a bootlace. The tendency then is for

The Equestrian Age of Reason

little hands, in order to hold them at all, to become clenched and stiff with a corresponding tightening of the muscles of the forearm. In this condition one is well on the way to creating a classic pair of "mutton fists".

Two of these little bridles were fitted with, of all things, sheepskin nosebands! The sheepskin nose-band (Fig. 7) originated in America and was used on trotting horses as an anti-shadow or anti-shying device, and in this connection was probably of

Figure 7
Sheepskin noseband

some use; it then migrated to France and the race course, and in due course to this country. Adjusted high enough up the face I concede that it might be of some value, otherwise, apart from being able to distinguish one's horse if he is the only one wearing it, it is vastly over-rated and I suspect but dimly understood. For a child's pony it is just ludicrous.

I was of course bound to see the ubiquitous plastic-covered browband in all its bilious glory. I wondered how long it would be before we began to produce them with a row of alternate Beatles and electric guitars studded with sequins!

One wall was covered, apart from the lovelies, with the conventional Weymouth or double bridles. How many, I wondered, would be used with understanding. I fear too many are used as brakes without the rider appreciating that the origin of the head position, and of control, lies not with the bit but in the early training of the horse and our ability to control the motive power of the quarters by the engagement of the hocks through the seat and legs.

Two special orders attracted my attention; the first a gag bridle fitted with a strong noseband hanging with an equally stout standing martingale. Presumably they were to be used in conjunction, obviously by one for whom the age of reason was a long way off. A gag bridle is used to raise the head; and if a stiff poll and neck are to be avoided, should in any case be fitted with two pairs of reins: one on the ring of the bit itself, so that whilst the animal behaves himself one is employing the normal snaffle action; and one actually attached to the rounding which passes through the hole in the bit ring, and which is used when one wishes to indicate that the head should be raised smartly. This bridle had but this latter rein, and the bit would therefore produce an accentuated head-raising effect. Why then, if this is the object, exert a contradictory downward force by using a martingale? It may produce more control at the expense of the animal's comfort, but it is completely illogical.

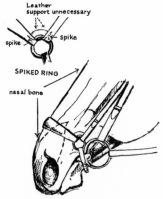

Figure 8 Correct fitting of Dropped Noseband

Next to the door hung a dozen or more drop-nosebands (Fig. 8). Innocent enough in appearance, and yet an article which provokes more uninformed criticism than most.

It is accused of restricting the breathing; of even being the cause of broken wind (this latter is quite nonsensical and is far more likely to be caused by a misused double bridle forcing the nose on to the chest), neither of which it does if properly fitted. The correct position is for the nosepiece, which should be secured to the head by means of a spiked ring and a piece of leather fitted between the two to prevent it dropping downwards, to be fitted some 3″ above the nostril (see Fig. 8), where it will not affect the breathing. It is, however, important that the rear strap fastening under the bit is long enough to allow for this positioning. In this position it is an admirable auxiliary to the snaffle bit bringing the head down by the pressure exerted on the nose, closing the mouth and therefore preventing a common evasion and so giving more control.

The last items I passed as I left the shops were a number of stable rollers,

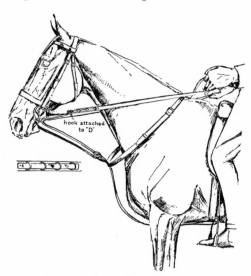

Figure 9 The Market Harborough rein (German rein)

a bundle of running martingales and a few Market Harborough martingales (Fig. 9).

The rollers were mainly of the conventional type with one or two of the arch anti-cast rollers. Their life will be a long one, and it is unlikely that we shall see them in for repair for many years. I don't like repairs, but I would welcome the sight of a few more rollers coming in at the end of the season to have the pads re-stuffed, if only that it would save me a great deal of time later on and a number of horses from getting sore backs. Most people would be horrified to see a saddle so badly stuffed that it put pressure on either backbone or withers, and yet so many will use rollers the pads of which have long since gone flat and in consequence exert a constant pressure for nearly twenty-four hours of the day on these very places. Quite 40 per cent of sore backs could be avoided if rollers received the same attention as saddles. My own preference is for the arch roller which, apart from being a deterrent against the animal getting cast, allows the backbone complete freedom providing of course the arch fits the back. The safest way of ensuring that it does in fact fit is to employ an adjustable hinged arch, as illustrated (Fig. 10), which can be used on either a narrow or a broad back.

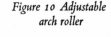

Figure 10 Adjustable arch roller

The running martingales were to go to a training stable, and in due course I expect to see them pass my breakfast-room window as the string makes its way to the gallops. Quite half of them will be hanging down around the horse's knees for want of making the correct adjustment, which would assist the rider in keeping the head down.

It always puzzles me as to why the Pulley Martingale (Fig. 11) is not more popular. For schooling, particularly over fences where quick turns are necessary, it must surely have great value. The sliding action of the rings allows the head and neck to be bent in the required direction without the restriction against the opposite side of the mouth (i.e. the offside when making a left-handed turn, and vice versa), which must be exerted with the ordinary pattern of martingale.

The Market Harborough (Fig. 9) is another unjustly maligned article. Apart from the fact that it is now beginning to lose its honest English name and to be called the "German" rein (in Germany it is known as the

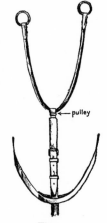

Figure 11

"English" rein), its use is banned in jumping competitions in the country of its origin.

It is in fact an improvement on the old type of draw rein (still permitted) which passed from the girth through the rings of the bit and directly to the rider's hand. The Market Harborough is not operated by the rider but rather by the horse raising his head when the strips of leather passing through the bit rings naturally tighten to produce a downward effect. The horse cannot become overbent as in the case of the old draw rein, and the device in no way restricts the extension of head and neck.

In my view if the Market Harborough is to be declared illegal, then logically you should also ban the very tight running martingale used with possibly a twisted snaffle.

My last call was on the Repair Shop, inevitably a depressing sight. Mounds of dirty rags, masquerading as rugs, row upon row of elderly saddles, and the usual hotchpotch of head collars, bridles, muzzles and the like. Most of this dilapidated tack belonged to racing stables, and all had the inevitable scarlet ticket marked MOST URGENT, TOMORROW and so forth. To undertake the repair of this sort of stuff is to bestow a favour, and yet the majority of trainers would hardly view repairs in this light.

Once, in my youth, when I still cherished hopes of changing the established order, I spent many hours putting to paper statistics on repairs for a very notable trainer. By going through his account for three years I proved that he was in fact wasting money which he could have saved had he implemented a system whereby he threw out the very old tack at the beginning of the year and replaced with new. The saving he could have effected would have been in the region of £200-£300 p.a., for there were numerous instances of saddles (often 40 years old) which in the space of a year had been in for repair as much as five times. In these cases the cost of repairs exceeded the cost of a new saddle, and he was still left with a 40-year-old saddle, which is hardly the sort of thing one would have thought was either worthy of or safe for an expensive thoroughbred.

I suspect the product of much midnight oil burning went straight to the waste paper basket; certainly there was no change in his repairs account.

Saddlery properly cared for and even when neglected lasts a long time, but why anyone should think it should be as indestructible as Methuselah (who might well have used some of the saddles I know) seems to me at best unreasonable.

By the time my day had finished I felt I had deserved my pre-dinner drink;

The Equestrian Age of Reason

on this occasion I filled my glass and prepared to down its contents with a silent toast to the coming of the equestrian age of reason in its entirety. Before the glass reached my lips, however, the toast had changed—"To my customers who may order everything illogically, but who nevertheless provide the wherewithal for my nightly glass!"

Better to hunt in fields for health unbought,
Than fee the doctor for a nauseous draught.
DRYDEN

A perfect horseman knows neither fear nor anger.
Some people tell you they ride by "balance" others by "grip". I think a man
might as well say he played the fiddle by "finger", or by "ear". Surely in
either case a combination of both is required to sustain the performance with
harmony and success.
G. J. WHYTE MELVILLE

Heavy hands make hard-mouthed horses.
JOHN ADAMS, 1799

If the man's heart is in the right place, his horse will seldom fail him; and
were we asked to name the one essential without which it is impossible to attain
proficiency in the saddle, we should not hesitate to say "nerve".

Everyone who rides does well to have a whip, stick, or crop in their hands, but
it should seldom be used as a means of punishment.
LIEUT.-COLONEL M. F. MCTAGGART

But there is one rule to be inviolably observed above all others; that is, never
to approach the horse in a passion; for anger never thinks of consequences, and
forces us to do what we afterwards repent.
Translated from the original Greek: XENOPHON'S TREATISE ON
HORSEMANSHIP, 400 B.C.

Clear Round

LIEUT.-COLONEL J. HUME DUDGEON, O.B.E., M.C.

IN THE OLD DAYS of cavalry, when I joined, one of the many things that was instilled into me was that The Horse was one's best friend. Although I fully agreed, how little I realised what a friend he was going to be! I have been privileged to be with horses, very closely connected with them, all my life, and it is quite impossible to describe the very great pleasure they have given me. And apart from that I have to thank the horse for taking me to a great many countries, and so seeing the world.

Up to 1907, which was the year that the International Horse Show started in London, there was not very much show jumping in England. However, even in the early 1900s I personally never missed the jumping in the Royal Dublin Society's Shows. The entries were good, the course consisted of six permanent fences, each one having a most delightful approach, the ground rising one foot in the last twenty. I always say that the fences were so long that one could easily have taken a troop of cavalry over them in line. Each fence had a privet hedge making a wing, with strong rails running out at least twenty feet from the fence. The competitors went in pairs. To the best of my recollection, no horse in those days was kept for show jumping only. They were all primarily hunters and show jumping was a very secondary consideration. These fences were laid out in such a way that the hunter had little difficulty in negotiating them. Even to well on in the 'twenties at Dublin Horse Show, hunters being judged in championships had to jump several of these permanent fences, usually "hedge and ditch" and the big "double bank".

The Spaniards ride with dash, and are always attractive to watch: Captain L. Sureda Moner on Ixion

Clear Round

After the First World War a good many people started taking show jumping seriously and to study the art. We young cavalry officers all had an excellent grounding in our regiments, and the lucky ones, again, in the Cavalry School at Netheravon and later on at the famous Army Equitation School at Weedon. I consider we were lucky having Colonel Rodzianko in England. He must be regarded as just about the most famous horseman and equitation instructor of this century. Apart from being such a fantastic instructor, his generosity knew no bounds. He was prepared to help anybody, though curiously enough the number who were wise enough to accept his help remained limited.

The chief object of this article is to endeavour to try to help the present generation a little with their show jumping, and if I can succeed, it will give me great satisfaction. Remember, when you take up show jumping, you are not only going to enjoy, I hope, jumping many clear rounds, but you are also going to have great satisfaction in training your horse. I think to be a really good show jumping rider and trainer of show jumping horses, one must be a very accomplished all-round horseman.

We must study horse psychology as well as conformation and, lastly, we must make a study of his training. The show jumping horse needs to be as handy as a polo pony, clever as a cat and brave as a lion! Most people are inclined to think that it is only the very exceptional horse who has the ability to become a show jumper. It is my belief that there are far more horses which can be produced into international jumping than people realise. I am afraid many horses suffer from lack of training and so we never hear of them. The well-made, well-balanced, attractive horse is the one which we want to find, and perhaps even more important, we want him to have a kind eye. It is surprising how often it works out that the horse with the kind eye has the right temperament.

The horse is *not* a natural jumper. He has to learn a technique and style. He has a great weight to lift, and having eighteen pairs of ribs he does not have much room between pelvis and ribs to bring up his hind legs. The cat and dog have the advantage over him in that the dog has only thirteen pairs of ribs and the cat only eleven. They are also luckier in their tendons and shock absorbers. So we must realise his difficulties. He has *not* a great brain and, therefore, the trainer must always remember that he, the trainer, must be clever and make things absolutely clear and be quite certain that the horse understands what he is being asked to do. He is such a very willing animal he will do the job if he has it explained right and really understands, and if the aid is quite definite. One must study each horse as an individual—some being sensitive and excitable—some lethargic and slow to respond. Temperament is all important and one can very often take a good gamble

ans Winkler on Halla: a truly great pair from Germany. Calm, cool,
terly efficient, with brilliance to help when the heat is on

on the horse's breeding and to a certain extent on his eye and general expression.

Conformation, of course, is worth studying and a well-made horse, good mover and well balanced, is a good start. But, curiously enough, the good points of a horse are always pointed out to you when he is successful. When they are not going well one is often told many bad points of horse conformation. So do remember the trainer really, to a very great extent, makes the horse. When people see a horse winning they say how lucky that owner seems to be! They do *not* seem to realise it is not all luck—it is training.

A good example of training was the Irish Army Jumping Team 1928/39, trained by Colonel Paul Rodzianko. They were a superb team, men and horses being examples of what is required. These great riders all agree that it was quite fantastic what Colonel Paul could do with man and horse. Throughout those eleven years they were right at the top of international jumping. Their stable consisted of about thirty horses, from which to choose their team of eight or ten. Nearly all these horses were purchased between the ages of four and five. It would seem this was a good example of what can be done. Colonel Borwick, who did so much for riding in Great Britain, used to say, "A strong horseman may force his horse into obedience, but to a rider who loves and understands him, in time he gives himself entirely." Keep your horse happy, work in such a way that he will enjoy his work and you will find the happy horse is the successful one, who will in time give himself entirely to you.

We give our early jumping lessons on lunge line. From this we gain the horse's confidence and it gives him experience, practice and variety of obstacles. He gets so handy on the lunge we even take him through the country and so he jumps what he will meet hunting. If he is a little slow, then when you start to ride him, let him sling along fast once or twice going at water. This gives him courage, which will be noticed over other fences afterwards. Having done so much on the lunge he has learnt the correct style and technique. Also, you will have seen exactly how the horse jumps; his approach, his take-off, period of suspension, his landing and his getaway. During these first stages he has balanced himself by use of head and neck. Horses jump with certain success in all styles, but the one who does it correctly does it with minimum effort.

Let us briefly go through the stages: (a) as he approaches and sees his jump ahead, he lowers his head, balances himself, arranges his stride, we see his ears cocked, and his concentration is all on his jump; (b) arriving at the spot from which to take off, his head comes in that little, the forehand is thrust up by forelegs, and at the same time hind feet come forward to the same spot at which the front ones left the ground; and the hind legs propel the horse forward over the jump; (c) during the jump, he stretches his head and neck to bring up his hind quarters and arches his back; (d) as he is coming down to land, his head comes up somewhat and his forelegs touch the ground he again thrusts them up and hind ones come in and push him forward; (e) he gets away, and is going on again at a normal, cadenced pace.

From the above I think we can see the importance of head and neck. And so we must remember, our hand must be elastic to allow this movement. But we must remember that although our hand is elastic, we must keep contact with his mouth. If you drop his head he loses his balance, you lose control and he can refuse. This applies to lunge line as well as rein when riding. The Cavesson head collar is best for lunging, but if you are in wide open spaces, your horse rather strong, and perhaps you not too strong, attach lunge line to bit for safety purposes. If you know your job, you will not do his mouth any harm. One of the advantages of lunging is we can do it anywhere. The long free lane, which we used to see so often, was very expensive to erect. The circular manège costs money too, but for lunge, all we want are four upright stands and a few poles. These can be erected anywhere, either in a quarter of an acre or a hundred acre park!

It is good to have several jumps over which you can lunge, but you need an assistant to keep arranging jumps as you wish. Remember, you must introduce your young horse to each jump, making it as easy and attractive as possible. We do not wish him to know he can stop! The man with lunge is much like a man on the horse's back, he must be quick to know when to give that extra sign to the horse to keep going. He must be equally clever when the horse is inclined to rush, and quieten him by decreasing pace, use of voice and, if he is really clever, by moving forward—*but* be careful, or you may very easily stop him and give him a bad habit.

I used to demonstrate making a horse increase his pace, decrease his pace, without whip or voice, merely by my own movement, by taking a pace to right or left—this was with a horse I had lunged over quite long periods. The horse is very observant, and you want to make full use of this. He will become calm and so be 100 per cent concentrated on his job. The wildest of horses, that rush their fences, can very easily be slowed down on the lunge. My favourite jump for lunging is parallel bars up to about 2′ 9″ and out to a spread of 7′. We, of course, start with spread of 18″, and very gradually increase, day by day, inch by inch. The horse that jumps these parallels soon learns to jump straight fences. During our period of lunging over jumps our horse has shown us what he can do. Even the lazier horse, now and then on lunge, finds himself awkwardly placed, and so as to save the trouble of making a serious error and hurting himself, he puts in a big effort and we see that he can jump.

Clear Round

One cannot improve on the standard and syllabus laid down in the cavalry for a troop horse. At the Italian Cavalry School they had a large manège with a cross jump in the middle, and they used to spend very long periods cantering round, changing direction, getting closer and closer to the jump and eventually jumping it. This is an exercise to be recommended, as it teaches horse and rider cadence of pace, has a calming effect on the horse and he soon learns to arrange himself and meet the jump correctly.

If you are lucky enough to live in a hunting country, take your horse out hunting all you can. This will open up a new world for him. He sees masses of other horses, has long hours out of stable which will really settle him down. Best of all he learns to be clever. He meets all kinds of fences. For "stake and bounds" with ditch to you, he must get close or he will not make it. If it's a post and rails with ditch to you, that will be an even worse disaster, if he stands too far away. But this will *not* happen with you because you have lunged him over so many fences, you have ridden him over many—you know each other—and, between you, the approach is such that you do *not* make any error and arrive at the right spot for take off without any undue fuss or change of pace. It is an excellent thing to take him across undulating ground. I am a great believer in teaching horses to go down really steep places. This helps their balance and, I consider, their courage. We teach him evenness of pace, lots of circling, changing direction and so on. I have a glen near our school in which I have made masses of little tracks along which one may trot or canter, with small fences here and there. This, I believe, is a great help in teaching the horse balance and change of direction. In fact, make your potential show jumper a really good riding horse, one who understands obeying hand and leg, and one who can quickly change direction. Take him into all bank country that you can find. Nothing is so good for the horse to learn the approach, as banks. This form of obstacle also teaches him to be clever in that if it is a narrow topped one, he really has to be rather cat-like: (a) to avoid flying over and landing in ditch on far side; (b) to get hind legs on top or just on the far side of the bank to push off and so clear the ditch. Most people advise keeping your young horse back in the crowd out hunting. Now, if you are a fox hunter, what a trial for you! No need to miss that great joy of being with hounds, and I find the young horse goes more quietly up with hounds than stuck back three fields behind, in the crowd! As Mr. Jorrocks said, "The horse loves the hound and I love both."

When you go to buy a horse there is no good in being too particular about his conformation, and one must be prepared to accept, anyhow to a certain extent, what the owner tells one. Should the people concerned read what I am about to say, I hope they will forgive me. The horse in question was one named "The Quiet Man", whom I only had for a few months. He was the most delightful horse but very plain. When these people arrived in my stable rather unexpectedly, the horse was not looking his best and they had one look and quickly went out of the stable saying they were not interested in that type. At the time I happened to have about four or five very good jumping horses and they returned to see these horses in action, the following morning. Needless to say, "The Quiet Man", whom they had turned down the night before, now with his main plaited, rather well ridden and jumping a few spectacular fences, quickly took their eye and they wisely purchased this horse who within one year must have been acknowledged to be one of the most famous show jumpers in the world. He had the athletic ability.

Now, how do we acquire our jumper? If one is very lucky, one may have one or two brood mares. As in racing, one can breed horses suitable for show jumping. There is tremendous satisfaction in breeding, training and bringing a horse into Grade "A" show jumping. If one does not breed horses oneself, one can buy the young horse, whose appearance and breeding look like producing the jumper. Those who have not got such patience and want to go to the top in a hurry will have quite a job in buying the horse who shows form. In my position as a Riding Establishment Director, I am continuously asked for show jumpers, and nine times out of ten, people will only buy the horse who has proved himself to be really exceptional.

And one final word of advice—the best horses come from Ireland!

There is no secret so close as that between a rider and his horse.

R. S. SURTEES, 1803–1864

A little neglect may breed mischief, . . . for want of a nail, the shoe was lost; for want of a shoe the horse was lost; for want of a horse the rider was lost.

BENJAMIN FRANKLIN, 1758

The aim of training a horse is to make him quiet, supple, and obedient by systematic work, so that he becomes pleasant in his movements and comfortable for his rider.

GUERINIERE

The horse must obey with the proud obedience of the soldier.

LORD WAVELL

Chestnut and Gumbo

One Day on a Ranch in Montana

DIANA WAINMAN

MY FIRST GLIMPSE of the cow pony destined to carry me was from inside a Jeep careering across some very rough country. We had covered a lot of ground looking for the horses, and finally found them in a sheltered gully conveniently close to a corral. As my host turned the Jeep blowing his horn, the horses cantered off uphill. They seemed a rough-looking collection. Bringing up the rear was a chestnut filly with wild eyes and a face like a camel. Bill, accelerating after them, said casually, "She will carry you well. She's young but very sensible." His two sons, Billy Jr. and John, aged ten and eight respectively, jumped off the back to head off the horses. After a great deal of exercise taken by both boys and horses, the latter were shut in the corral.

I had arrived at the ranch late the night before and had had little time to look around. However, I realised that any preconceived ideas I had about cowboys and their mounts were all wrong. Naïvely, I had always imagined that when a cowhand wanted his horse, he whistled and along came the horse. All in the best tradition of cowboy films no doubt, but useless on this particular ranch. Bill E. Benson, my host, had explained that compared to the big cattle ranches his acreage was small—only twenty-three thousand acres. His horses were purely for working purposes, and broken by him in his spare time. As he ran the ranch with the help of one hired man, his wife, and three children, it was obvious that there was little, if any, spare time for anyone.

Bill and the two boys disappeared into the mob of horses in the corral

Chestnut and Gumbo

and reappeared leading my chestnut, a large roman-nosed bay, and two ponies. If the first impression of my mount had been unencouraging, the second was worse. As I walked up to her, making what I thought were happy, horse-sounding noises, she reared several times. Then, determined to show me how unwelcome I was, she made a very determined, and almost successful, attempt to bite me. I retreated hastily, bitterly regretting having left the comfort and civilisation of the Eastern seaboard. Bill, callously indifferent to my nervousness, shouted to me to stop wasting time and fetch the saddle. I ran back to the Jeep to fetch it. The boys had already saddled their ponies and were working with their father's horse, so only mine was left. Accustomed to an ordinary English hunting saddle, I thought the western one looked like something from the middle ages. I was not surprised to be told later that it weighed around forty pounds. Staggering back with the saddle, blanket, bridle and rope, I thought with relief that at least the horse could not possibly buck under the accumulated load, as well as my not inconsiderable weight.

Mounting was easy. The long box stirrups hung down so far that very little spring was needed. Once in the saddle I felt secure, if rather uncomfortable. The great rounded knob on the pommel was far more satisfying to cling on to than any neck-strap. I began to feel more cheerful. However, I discovered only too quickly that communication between myself and the pony was non-existent. Gentle pressure with the right rein and left leg in the approved pony club style made no impression at all. The boys, mounted and cantering easily in tightening circles, were rather scornful. "Don't you English know how to ride?" from John did nothing to help. Billy Jr. taking pity on me, explained that if I neck-reined and leant outwards in the direction I wanted to go, maybe I would manage. It certainly worked, although it felt somewhat like riding a motor bicycle.

Bill, having released the remaining horses from the corral, swung easily onto his horse, which promptly gave a bucking display, which for speed and elegance far outshone any rodeo film. He just sat there, holding his pommel with one hand, and laughed. I was suitably impressed until Billy Jr. riding his pony close to mine, murmured, "Dad's horse always does that for strangers!"

We set off at a slow canter towards the cattle pastures. Although it was early April, the day was warm. As we topped each little hill we could see for miles. The country, although treeless and almost waterless, is attractive. The long greyish-brown grass is broken by patches of rock, and cement-like mud, called gumbo. In places the hills fall away in steep cliffs, broken by long gullies or draws. Except for the breeze rippling through the long grass, the silence is complete.

Chestnut and Gumbo

After an hour of steady riding we came to a wire fence. On the near side of it eleven enormous bulls were grazing. They looked placid enough, but I was not sorry when we made a detour to the gate in the fence. Bill sent John off by himself. He looked tiny as he disappeared up a draw between two hills. I asked Bill where the boy had gone. He said he had told him to ride up the fence for two miles, and then cut across country to join us. It semed to me more than probable that an eight-year-old child would get lost, but I didn't say anything.

As we rode on Bill explained that all the cows calving were in this pasture. Since they were all branded with a number it would be easy to check on them. All new calves were ear-tagged and had paste put on their horn buttons to prevent growth. Bill said that during the calving season it was wise to check at least once every day: some cows had trouble and needed help while several were bad mothers. Frankly the thought of acting midwife at a calf's delivery did not appeal.

Billy Jr. was riding a little ahead, swinging his rope, when he pulled up and pointed to the right. Below us there was a dip in the ground and in it was a cow with a new-born calf, which was struggling to its feet. Bill leapt off, ran down to the calf and brought it down in a flying tackle just as it was moving off. He sat astride it and proceeded to tag it. He was putting paste on its horns when the cow, who had been watching from a little way off, began to make vicious noises. She started to move in towards him in a menacing fashion. Billy Jr. grabbed his father's horse and took it over to him. Bill pulled the calf right underneath his horse, and calmly finished the operation. The calf, released, wobbled off unsteadily to rejoin its mother, who, having examined her baby for injury, led it away. Bill remounted, and while we watched the cow and calf moving off he explained that many of the cows became fierce at times, but that they would not come too close to your horse.

Looking around, I realised Billy Jr. had vanished. Bill shrugged, and said, "He's capable. He'll work back to us." We rode on. Bill tagged several more calves without incident. I was rather disappointed not to see him use the rope. He said that there were quite a number of larger calves that he had missed the week before, which would have to be roped; but that there was no point in roping calves which could easily be caught. It all looked so simple I asked if I could deal with the next one. This was a grave error. Having run for what seemed miles in my borrowed boots after the most elusive animal, I managed to grab a hind leg. I then realised that the calf, although so small, was a lot tougher than it looked, and it was only with great difficulty that I managed to hold it down. It was as slippery as an eel, and about as awkward to hold. Having finally dealt with it, I remounted very breathless and rather pleased with myself. Bill effectively cast a damper by

Chestnut and Gumbo

saying, "If the boys took as long as you, I'd curse them." Then, seeing my crestfallen face, added, "Not too bad for a girl, and a beginner at that."

As we rode over the next hill, we heard shouts. Billy Jr. was riding his skewbald pony flat out in pursuit of a well-grown calf. Bill reined in his horse, pushed his hat to the back of his head and said, smiling, "Watch this. It's for your benefit. The lad's not strong enough to hold a big calf yet. I think he's going to find this tough!"

Billy's pony was gaining on the calf. As we watched, he swung his rope, aimed and missed. The calf shied away and turned towards us. His second try was successful, the noose landed squarely over the calf's head. The pony, by far the more experienced of the two, pulled up sharply. Billy Jr. was not quick enough to take a turn with the end of the rope around the pommel. The calf, momentarily halted by the jerk of the rope, started off again. The rope end slipped out of his hand. He managed to jump off and grab the rope's end, but was pulled off his feet by the calf. He hung on grimly, it was a fairly even battle. After a great deal of effort he managed to sit on the calf's head. From this rather precarious position, he shouted for help. We rode over to him, suppressing laughter. Billy Jr. scarlet in the face, panted, "Gee, Dad, this one's a tough little bastard. I showed him who's boss though." Then he turned to me and said, "I ought to have held him from my pony. Every now and then one gets away, even if you are used to it!"

Riding on, Bill explained that all good cow ponies are almost capable of doing their work unaided. He proved his point when we found about fifteen cows with calves in a sheltered gully. He rode down to them, showed his horse which calf he wanted; then dropped the reins on its neck and sat still. The horse slowly worked the calf to the edge of the group. The calf twisted and turned to try to rejoin the others. Every time the calf turned the horse cut it off, and in a few minutes the calf was well away from the rest with the horse in between. Bill tagged the calf and let it return to the others. I asked him how he trained the horse. He said that he didn't have time, but that this horse had cow sense. He bought his horses locally, tried them, and any that were useless were resold.

We stopped for lunch on the crest of a small hill. I took the heavy saddle off my pony and let her graze. She looked blown and rather tucked up. As we sat in the sun, Bill remarked, "She's done well, that filly. I only backed her last week." Grinning, he added, "I didn't tell you. I thought you might have been scared!" I said that, had I known, I would not have gone near her. He said, "I bought her a month ago, unbroken, but she seemed gentle enough. I wasn't too sure how she'd go for you. She never had a bit in her mouth before today." In my ignorance I had thought I was the only novice!

Sitting rather sleepily in the warm sun, I asked about the ranch. Bill told me that, being a near drought area, it took almost forty acres to feed every cow and calf; and that the grass, although so dead looking, was fairly high in food value. In the winter he supplemented grass with cake, fed from a tractor and trailer. He had a little arable land, and a few sheep. He made a certain amount of hay. This was the busiest time of the year, and bad weather could do a lot of damage. Indeed, the week before I arrived they had had fifteen inches of snow. The winter was often as cold as thirty degrees below zero, while the summer temperature could rise to above a hundred and five.

The ponies lifted their heads, Billy Jr.'s skewbald pony neighed. John, a mere speck in the distance, was cantering his pony towards us. We waited for him. Meanwhile Bill explained that the boys broke their own ponies and that John's grey was a great success; but that he had had to ride Billy Jr.'s himself to stop it bucking the child off. John arrived rather breathless, and, while eating his lunch, gave his father a detailed report of all he had seen. He reeled off a spate of numbers which Bill wrote down in a notebook. He seemed to have remembered the number, sex, and locality of a great many calves. I was impressed that an eight-year-old could be so responsible, but Bill took it as a matter of course. John's final piece of information was that there was one cow in trouble. He said she was obviously having difficulty calving, and looked ill. Bill decided to go and investigate.

We saddled up and rode westwards down a long winding trail between steep cliffs. The boys, riding some way ahead, were telling each other what they had done and seen. We came round a corner to see a level plain in front which looked like a dried up river bed. Just below us were several large patches of gumbo, interspersed with holes. Bill said they were washouts, caused by rain or melting snow rushing off the cliffs. A cow was wandering up and down, bellowing plaintively. Bill stopped the boys and watched for a few moments. He said, "That cow has lost her calf. Stupid to calve down here in all this mud, she should have had more sense." He got off his horse and walked down towards her. She watched him come, and moved off a little still bellowing. He stood for a minute, and then walked on looking in the holes. His horse moved slowly behind him, reins dragging. Suddenly the horse moved off to the left and stopped by a small washout. Bill went over, bent down, and with some difficulty hauled out a calf so covered in mud as to be barely recognisable. It had fallen head first down the hole, and stuck. It looked very small and weak and just lay where he put it. The cow approached warily and then, satisfied that this was her baby under all the mud, started to lick it clean. When the calf had got to its feet, we drove them both up the hill, well away from the mud-holes, and left them there.

We found John's cow near where he had seen her. She was by herself on the side of a grassy slope. Bill looked at her, then undid his rope. "She'll have to go to the vet.," he said. He glanced around, "She's in the worst place to get a trailer to. Not even a thorn bush to tie her to." He decided to rope her, then drive or lead her down the valley and fasten her to a stunted thorn bush, while he fetched the Jeep and trailer. By the time we had tied the unwilling animal to the bush, the sun had set. It was getting cold and I, for one, was very stiff and rather tired. "I'll have to go fetch the Jeep. It'll take an hour or two," said Bill, then, glancing at the cow, "I don't like to leave her." Rather horrified at the idea of being left alone, I rashly volunteered to stay with her till he got back. Fortunately Billy Jr. offered to stay with me. I was delighted to have company, but as Bill and John rode off into the dusk, I felt like calling them back. Billy Jr., however, appeared unmoved and, having cast an eye over the cow who was standing quietly, proceeded to unsaddle his pony.

I could not show myself nervous in front of a ten-year-old child, so I followed suit. Billy stood his saddle upright in a hollow; then he lay down between the two saddle blankets, using the upright saddle as a makeshift bed-head, and promptly went to sleep. Except for the ponies grazing, the heavy breathing of the poor cow, and occasional small snores from Billy Jr., the silence was absolute. It had become dark and the sky, spangled with thousands of stars, seemed vast. Suddenly the silence was split by a blood curdling howl. To say that I was startled and frightened is an under statement. The ponies flung up their heads and snorted uneasily. Billy Jr. sat up, then rolled over muttering, "Damn coyote. I'll tell Dad to bring the gun out tomorrow." He was fast asleep again almost at once.

We waited for what seemed eternity. Twice I had to go to move the cow who seemed determined to strangle herself. Billy Jr. slept on. At last, away in the distance, I heard the roar of the Jeep. They had brought a flask of much-needed whisky for me, and some cake for the ponies, which we fed and turned loose. Getting the cow into the trailer was not easy, but after half an hour of pushing and struggling, the exhausted animal finally climbed the ramp.

We then drove more than sixty miles to get to the vet., mostly on dirt roads. I will not go into details of what happened there, but a Caesarian with the cow still on its feet was not attractive. However, the cow did not appear to suffer unduly. Having left the cow in the vet.'s care, we finally got back to the ranch at two a.m. As I fell into bed I wondered whether every day was going to be as eventful as my first.

Coaching and Driving

MARYLIAN WATNEY

THE HISTORY of coaching has been written in many books, yet the subject is never boring, for there is something fascinating about learning of the adventures and dangers of travel in former ages, and coaching stories provide numerous anecdotes, both thrilling and amusing.

Although the first recorded amateur coachman was Charles I, followed by Oliver Cromwell, who promptly had an accident, it was not until Regency days, when the roads had been so considerably improved by Telford and Macadam, that the art of driving horses graduated from a method of getting about to a fashionable pastime for young bloods. Four-in-hand driving in particular fired them with enthusiasm, so that many young men began bribing the professional coachmen into letting them have "a handful". This was of course not allowed officially for safety reasons, but fortunately the rule was often broken, and posterity has thus been supplied with many stories of the coaching days by the authors of diaries and journals.

Lord Algernon St. Maur recorded in the Badminton book *Driving* that he drove many coaches, including the Gloucester Mail, which left Oxford at 11 p.m. and arrived in London at 6 a.m., when he retired to bed for two hours, after which he spent the day as usual. He preferred, he said, to drive at night as "the horses were always so lively, and to hear the ring of their feet on a sharp frosty night, the rattle of the bars and the clatter as they rose and surmounted the tops of the hills, was to me the sweetest of music". He told also of an occasion when he was driving from London down Henley Hill when the professional coachman sitting beside him began "chirping" at the horses which started them pulling. Next he warned Lord Algernon that it was a nasty hill with a bridge at the bottom, but that they must get along,

"*Coach Match against Time*": James Selby driving the Old Times coach or epic run from London to Brighton and back in under eight hours
From a painting by H. Bird, 1

"*The Four-in-Hand Club*"   From a painting by James Pollard

"*Good Company*"—*a Stage Coach and Cocking Cart*

Coaching and Driving

"only mind what you're at, as this is just the spot where my partner was killed this day week when he ran up a bank and turned the coach over". Small wonder that Lord Algernon decided to leave this road for Basingstoke and Exeter, which he said, he much preferred. Lord Algernon must, however, have been an exceedingly skilful whip, for he gives a lively account of an occasion when driving into Sudbury and he found a man wheeling a barrow in the middle of the road. Expecting him to move, it was with horror that he saw the man jump out of the way, but leaving the barrow where it was. As they had a heavy load and were travelling downhill, it was impossible to stop, so, with great presence of mind, he opened out the leaders and managed to clear the barrow with the horses, though it was smashed to atoms when the coach wheel caught it.

Accidents of course make thrilling stories, and some of these were either so unusual or so graphic that they were depicted by artists of the day. The great snowstorm of 1836, for instance, which prompted James Pollard, Henry Alken and many others into painting scenes of mail coaches stuck helplessly in deep snow are frequently reproduced as Christmas cards today. The great snowstorm also produced tales of great courage on the parts of coachmen and guards, whose loyalty to the Post Office caused them considerable suffering in their efforts to look after and deliver the mail bags under their care. Another famous mishap, also painted by James Pollard, shows the leader of the Exeter mail coach being attacked by an escaped lioness from a travelling menagerie. This occurred in 1816 outside the Pheasant Inn at Winterslow on Salisbury Plain, and undoubtedly caused a great sensation at the time, though it is happily recorded that the horse recovered from its wounds and lived for many years afterwards. Other accidents occurred through coaches racing each other, breakages of axles, coach wheels, or harness, horses shying or running away, and of course through the dangers of driving in fog, but on the whole it was surprising that there were not more of them.

Most of the horses used for coaching were a mixed lot. From race-horses, hunters, or gentlemen's carriage horses which had developed bad habits or had broken knees—anything in fact on four legs which would go. The night coaches were the worst horsed, and the old saying of "three blind 'uns and a bolter", used by coachmen to describe a rough team, often held true. Blind horses were, however, considered perfectly safe for night driving and some coachmen even preferred them. The big yards in London and the outskirts stabled between 1500 and 2000, and at one time their lives as coachhorses was not reckoned to be longer than three years. The smart, crack coaches, horsed by the bigger proprietors did, however, take a pride in producing better teams, and some of the amateur whips commented favourably on these. Some coach horses developed strange idiosyncrasies, such as the grey leader at Hounslow, who always refused to start unless he had ear caps on. Lord Algernon St. Maur, who records this, wondered very much how this peculiar demand was ever discovered, for it was not the age of pandering to horses. Another horse, sold for £10 because he jibbed so badly in a gentleman's carriage, went perfectly in a team when there was no bearing rein. Some horses could only be driven on either the near or the off side. But perhaps the most poignant story was of the attractive little brown mare who, it was rumoured, "knew her own way about Tattersall's yard", having been sold there so many times. At last she found a buyer who was determined to keep her, and who, when he discovered that she had been involved in a bad accident which probably accounted for her refusal to go in harness, decided to breed from her.

With so many keen young amateur coachmen about, one or two driving and coaching clubs were soon formed. The first was the B.D.C. known alternatively as the Bedfont, Benson, or Bensington Driving Club. This was formed in 1807 and limited to twenty-five members who drove twice a year from London to the Black Dog at Bedfont, near Hounslow—a distance of fourteen miles, or to the White Hart, Bensington, near Oxford, which was fifty-six miles away. This club was also known as the Black and White Club on account of its two destinations being the *Black* Dog and *White* Hart. The Black Dog at Bedfont appears, however, to have been the Club's head-quarters, for they kept their wine cellar there; while Bensington was near the home of one of their members, Sir Henry Peyton, famous for his team of greys. After the B.D.C. came the Benevolent Whip Club, which was subscribed to by all driving men in order to help professional coachmen and guards who were in distress.

The popularity of the B.D.C. soon produced the need for another club, and this was formed in 1808 by Mr. Charles Buxton, the inventor of the Buxton bit, and called the Four Horse Club, and sometimes though apparently wrongly, known as the Four-in-Hand Club or the Barouche Club. The Badminton book *Driving* describes their vehicles as being *Vis* Landaus, a larger version of the little vis-à-vis which held only two people sitting opposite to each other, while Lord William Pitt Lennox, in his book on anecdotes of the road, refers to them as Barouche-Landaus. At any rate, paintings of them show them as being more like canoe-shaped Landaus, which, with the hoods up, resembled the coaches they had become so attached to. Club rules insisted that the bodies of these carriages should be painted yellow, and that the horses drawing them should all be bays, though it is recorded that one member, Mr. Annesley, always drove roans. The Club also had its own uniform consisting of a drab-coloured coat reaching to the ankles with three tiers of pockets, and mother-of-pearl buttons the size of five-shilling pieces. The waistcoat was striped blue and yellow, with plush breeches tied with strings and rosettes at the knee, while the hats were wide-brimmed, and 3½ inches deep in the crown.

Whereas members of the B.D.C. drove to Bedfont or Bensington, the Four Horse Club always met at Mr. Buxton's house in Cavendish Square and drove to Salt Hill, near Maidenhead, patronising either the Windmill, or Castle hotels there, and great rivalry sprang up between these two hostelries for the honour of serving the Four Horse Club's dinners. For several years these two driving clubs flourished, but in 1815 the Four Horse Club began to fail and was disbanded in 1820. An attempt to revive it was then made in 1822, but this was finally given up in 1824. The B.D.C. meantime continued, though in 1824 they gave up the long journey to Bensington, but continued to Bedfont where, on one occasion, King George IV arrived to change horses on his way to Windsor, and they were able to drink his health "with three times three".

Despite the failure of the Four Horse Club in 1824, 1838 saw the formation of the Richmond Driving Club. This was founded by the Earl of Chester-field, who was determined to end the fashion of apeing the manners and dress of stage-coachmen, and insisted that his members "looked like gentle-men, but drove like coachmen". This club held their dinners at the Castle Hotel on the Thames at Richmond, but lasted for only six or seven years, when the B.D.C. was once again the sole survivor until 1854 when, due to the increasing age of its members, it was finally wound up. 1856 and the end of the Crimean war saw, however, the birth of yet another club. This was the Four-in-Hand Driving Club, presided over by the Duke of Beau-fort, and limited to thirty members. These began by meeting at 5 p.m. in Hyde Park to drive to the Castle at Richmond for dinner, but there was such a strong protest about ensuing traffic jams that they were asked either to change the times of their meets or else to meet elsewhere. They accordingly agreed to use the Horse Guards Parade ground, and, apart from their dinners, also attended cricket at Lords, and racing at Ascot and other courses, where they were provided with special enclosures.

The Four-in-Hand flourished to such an extent that in 1883 the rules were amended into admitting fifty members, but this proved insufficient to the applications, so that in 1870 yet another overflow club was formed. This was called the Coaching Club, and also under the presidency of the Duke of Beaufort. From a start of fifty members the number soon increased to 120, when it was decided to limit the membership to one hundred. This Club had its first meet in June 1871 when twenty-two coaches, the largest num-ber ever mustered, assembled at Marble Arch to drive to the Trafalgar Hotel

Coaching and Driving

at Greenwich for dinner. The Club also produced its own livery, consisting of a dark (Beaufort) blue coat and buff wasitcoat with gilt buttons engraved "C.C."

Both the Four-in-Hand and its less exclusive junior partner the Coaching Club flourished, each holding two parades a year at either the Magazine in Hyde Park or else on Horse Guards Parade, when they drove down to Greenwich, Richmond, the Crystal Palace, Hurlingham, or Ranelagh Club for luncheon. The Four-in-Hand Club, however, gradually went into a decline, while the Coaching Club is still active today having thirty members who meet and drive their coaches to the two parades a year.

From the earliest coaching days, speed was of course considered the essential. The Post Office being the first to ensure that the Mail coaches both left and arrived promptly and to schedule. In order to regularise the timing in every part of the country, the coach Guards were provided with watches fitted into locked containers—the keys being kept by the authorities. Coachmen also prided themselves on the speed of their stages, and one coach in particular, the Devonport Mail, or "Quicksilver" as it was nick-named, is said to have been one of the fastest coaches on the road. Another quick coach was the Exeter "Telegraph" on which Lord Algernon St. Maur travelled, stating that they left London at 5 a.m. and reached Exeter at 10.30 p.m.: 176 miles in $17\frac{1}{2}$ hours, changing horses twenty times. The amateur coachmen were of course also anxious to attain the speeds of the professionals, and one of Lord Algernon's friends once enquired of a professional his shortest time driving a four-mile stage between Wincanton and Last Gate. "Fifteen minutes," was the reply. "I think it might be done in twelve," ventured the amateur, and putting the horses into a gallop, he did the four miles in just under the time.

As a result of the desire for the conquest of speed, many wagers were taken up by young men of the day. Perhaps the most famous event in coaching history was the historic run from London to Brighton and back in under eight hours made by James Selby in 1888. Driving the "Old Times" coach (which is now in the possession of Messrs. Bertram Mills Circus), James Selby, who was a professional coachman during the coaching revival period, was wagered £1,000, forfeiting £500 if he failed, to drive from Hatchett's Restaurant in Piccadilly to the Old Ship Hotel in Brighton and back in under eight hours. The proposed run received a great deal of publicity, and it is recorded that all London was agog with excitement when the morning of 13 July dawned. Police had been detailed to clear the traffic if need be, and crowds were gathering along the road and at the stops for changes of horses. Selby himself was full of confidence, as smiling happily he mounted the box and took the reins, and when he returned 7 hours 50 minutes later, having covered

Four-in-hand team of heavy draught horses: Messrs. Mann, Crossm and Paulin's team of shires driven by Mr. W. Potter

the 108 miles ten minutes under the specified time, he received a tumultuous welcome. Apart from having won his wager to cover the distance in the time, his grooms had at one stage produced a world record of changing horses in 48 seconds. This was later broken by the grooms to Miss Sylvia Brocklebank who managed to do it in 47 seconds; while at the Royal International Horse Show in 1960 the grooms to Messrs. Watney's Red Rover coach succeeded in changing horses in 45 seconds.

Selby's run to Brighton caused a stir in coaching circles for a long time, and then in 1891 Lord Lonsdale, the sporting peer, challenged the Earl of Shrewsbury and Talbot to another driving match against time. This was to consist of a five-mile stretch of road between a house near Reigate and the Sun Inn at Crawley, which was to be covered four times by different horses and methods of driving, so that the total twenty miles would be completed in under one hour. The first lap was to be covered with a single horse in harness; the return lap with a pair; the third lap with a four-in-hand; and the final return lap with a pair again, but ridden postilion this time. The point of the wager was to prove that thoroughbred horses galloping, which were Lord Lonsdale's choice, would give a superior performance of speed to the fast trotters favoured by Lord Shrewsbury. Lord Lonsdale went into strict training for the event, which was scheduled to take place in March, and once again the public's imagination was well and truly stirred. Weather conditions became very bad a few days before and there was a heavy fall of snow, but a snow-plough had been summoned to clear the road, a referee and other racing officials had volunteered to check the race at points along the road, when it became known that Lord Shrewsbury had abandoned the idea of attending. To disappoint not only himself but his many friends and supporters who had come to watch the match, was not in Lord Lonsdale's nature. He therefore decided to carry on by himself, but that his opponent should now be time only. At the stroke of 1 o'clock he was off at a gallop driving a 15·2 hand thoroughbred to a light American Buggy. The police, however, intervened by warning him that he was driving to the public danger, but they made no attempt to stop him. Then a mounted onlooker's horse jibbed across the road, and nearly caused an accident, but in spite of these two checks, he took under fourteen minutes to reach Crawley. There he spent three seconds changing from the Buggy to the almost equally light-weight pair-horse phaeton, and with his two 15·3 brown mares raced back along the road in under thirteen minutes. Within forty seconds he was out of the phaeton, and mounted on the high box-seat of the coach with his four-in-hand, the wheelers of which were ex-Fire Brigade horses, and the leaders throughbreds, and away at full gallop back to Crawley. Here he checked in in just over fifteen minutes, and having removed his great-coat and exchanged

Coaching and Driving

his bowler hat for a cap, he sped to the four-wheel buggy and mounted the near-side horse to drive the final lap home postilion, in under fourteen minutes. The waiting crowd went mad with excitement. Twenty miles done in 55½ minutes was a real road record, and Lord Lonsdale, covered in mud, but flushed with pleasure, was congratulated on all sides.

Apart from famous coaching and driving personalities of the past, the names of the horses which performed outstanding feats of speed or endurance have also been handed down, in either stories or portraits. The Maid of the Mill, for instance, who trotted twenty-eight miles in two hours over Sunbury Common in 1824, and who was painted by Sartorius. Then there was Creeping Sally, a blind pony, who was heavily backed to trot fifty miles within five hours. The route lay betweeen Shoreditch and Harlow, and when a thick fog developed, it had no effect upon Sally, who trotted happily and apparently without distress, arriving with sixteen minutes to spare. Other famous trotting horses were Lady from Birmingham, Phenomena from Norfolk, the American challenger Rattler, and Miss Turner from Wales.

With today's road conditions, it would be impossible to attempt driving records similar to those achieved in the past, and nor would present-day owners of horses and ponies wish to press them to this extent. Nevertheless, there are definite signs of a growing revival of interest in driving for pleasure. The Coaching Club of 1870 remains with us, and the five-year-old British Driving Society has members in every part of England. Carriages of all sorts: gigs, phaetons, dog-carts and rallis are being restored as lovingly as the harness is polished and the horses are groomed, and the art of driving elegantly and correctly is studied with the same care.

In 1831 Squire Osbaldeston for a bet rode 200 miles in 8 hours and 42 minutes, changing horses frequently during the journey, and said he could have ridden another 100 miles as he "was not in the least fatigued"!

Up a hill hurry not,
Down a hill flurry not,
On level ground spare him not.
ON A MILESTONE near Richmond, Yorks.

Three Days' Hard

SHEILA WILLCOX WADDINGTON

A THREE-DAY EVENT in itself is an exhausting business so it is only to be expected that the preparation involved is arduous and lengthy. Indeed, it occurs to me again and again that I must be completely mad to want to compete in Horse Trials at all.

The experts tell us that it takes a minimum of two years to train a potential Eventer from the unschooled novice to a horse ready for preliminary competitions. This, in itself, is hardly likely to attract great numbers of new riders to the ranks of Trialists; and even if one can persuade a likely person into considering the transition, there are more and more reasons why he will be likely to turn eventually to show jumping as the less arduous and more rewarding pursuit. Here I must say that I imply no criticism through the above remark to show jumping—quite the contrary. Had I a brilliant horse and the opportunity to range the countryside from April to October each year I might well be tempted to try my luck at this specialised branch of equestrianism. This, however, is out of the question and, instead, I concentrate on the Three-day Event which demands such obedience, stamina, courage and precision from both horse and rider that it necessitates long and arduous preparation.

Fitness both of horse and rider is of supreme importance in the Trials. It is no good having a superb jumper which one knows can negotiate any cross-country fence if he is not also going to be capable of remaining strong enough to complete the twenty-odd miles of a Three-day Event, or Olympic course, and still be ready to show jump next day. The Speed and Endurance Test of the second day in Horse Trials is not to be undertaken lightly. It

Three Days' Hard

demands great courage and perseverance on the part of the horse and considerable understanding of pace from the rider. Together they face an endurance test covering twenty miles which is divided into five phases run consecutively. The first is Roads and Tracks, where one completes four or five miles in a given time. There are no bonus marks to be gained for finishing within the time allowed, but one is penalised for exceeding the given time. Competitors may choose the pace at which they cover the phase and ride generally at a steady trot throughout or alternate between walk and canter. A competitor may even walk with his horse, but he must finish any one phase mounted.

The second phase is a steeplechase, but again it is an individual effort, and one competes against the clock rather than in the company of other horses. Here, one's judgment of pace tells. The steeplechase is over approximately twelve fences in two and a half miles and allows bonus marks to those who complete the phase within the time allowed, and penalises the horse who overlaps his allowed time. It is of the utmost importance throughout this phase to bear in mind the rigours of the remaining three phases and not to push one's horse too fast, only to find he has no more to give in the later stages. The end of the steeplechase phase brings one immediately on to Phase C, approximately seven miles of Roads and Tracks. Again it must be completed at the same speed as Phase A, but now one has covered already several miles, the latter part at a pace bound to tell on even the fittest horse. This fatigue will be very apparent as the horse starts on Phase C, and the wise will allow their horses a little time to recover breath before settling seriously to the long ride to the Cross Country. At the end of the Roads and Tracks there is a compulsory wait of ten minutes. This allows not only that the horse be rubbed over and prepared for the Cross Country but that he may be examined by a veterinary surgeon and committee who are empowered to eliminate any horse which shows signs of undue stress or strain. This is a recent innovation, the aim of which is to ensure that no unfit horse will start the cross country phase. Here the test is at its most severe, and a tired horse will make the fatal mistake only too easily. All the cross country fences, and there are thirty or more of them, are fixed and completely solid. There is no question of hitting a fence really hard and remaining upright. Either one clears the fence properly or runs the risk of turning head over tail in the unequal struggle against an immovable object. One needs a horse which will respect these fences. Not only this, but a horse of courage and stamina, able also to jump at awkward angles, up hill and down hill and into and out of water. He must have complete confidence in his rider and be so schooled that he is content to jump any fence, however forbidding, simply because of his rider's demands.

Calm confidence, and all goes w
Mrs. Waddington at Badminton

Elegance and poise: Mrs. Waddington on High and Mighty during the dressage phase of the 3 Day Event at Badminton, 1958

Stretched to the limit during the cross-country phase at Harewood: Miss A. Drummond-Hay on Perhaps

Three Days' Hard

Towards the end of this phase undoubtedly the strain of the distance covered will tell. The rider's judgement now becomes all important. He must not continue to drive his horse beyond its endurance, nor must he expect the horse to jump as effortlessly as at the start of the phase. The more experienced riders will have learned the speed their horses can maintain for the five miles and will not make the mistake of setting out at too hot a pace and then making a fatal error through exhaustion.

The last phase is simply a Run In on the Flat and is completed at a fast canter over a mile. It should act in the same way to the horse as the athlete's continued run after his effort of the race. It is an unwinding process, but still carries penalties for those who exceed the time allowed. This Run In concludes the Speed and Endurance Day. Obviously, it is this second day which has the greatest influence on the competition. It carries great penalties for exceeding the time allowed in any one of the five phases. It penalises falls either on the cross country or steeplechase at sixty points a time, and refusals up to the eliminating fourth at any one obstacle by twenty, forty, and sixty points, respectively. On the bonus side, completing the steeplechase and the cross country phases in minimum time can gain one over one hundred bonus points, though it is as well to remember that a speed faster than the minimum time allowed reflects bad judgement on the part of the rider and results only in unnecessary strain on the horse. The second day, then, can change completely the leading places from those of the Dressage Phase, and provides for some competitors the perfect excuse that it is unnecessary to perform a very good dressage test. In my opinion this is completely the wrong approach. The dressage phase is the only one for which one can train one's horse absolutely to the standard required. There really is no excuse for those who maintain their horses never could be any good at dressage. Any horse is capable of performing a fairly good test provided he has undergone systematic training, and it seems sheer stupidity not to take advantage of this fact. The training for dressage can only help both horse and rider in the future. It produces obedience to the aids, suppleness, and lightness. All these will become of enormous advantage in the second and third days' tests, and in addition to this a good dressage test places one among the leaders for the start of the Speed and Endurance. I maintain that, psychologically alone, this is of great importance. Why start the second day's test knowing one must redeem the marks lost through bad dressage? It means one must gain bonus marks in excess of all the competitors in the higher places. Undoubtedly, there will be those whose forte is the dressage alone and who are not able to complete the Speed and Endurance test without incurring severe penalties. On the other hand, one of those leaders may be capable of completing the second day's test not only without penalties but with maximum bonus marks, and in a case like this it becomes virtually impossible to overtake him. The man with the poor dressage score also sets out on the steeplechase and cross country phases to gain as many bonus points as possible. This is his only way of retrieving the lead, but it exposes him to the temptation of jumping too fast fences which otherwise he would approach more circumspectly. He courts danger unnecessarily and will fall the harder from the sheer force of greater speed.

Ideally, then, one requires a horse who will perform, consistently, a dressage test which will leave one up with the leaders. Then, he must be capable of completing the Speed and Endurance Phases without penalties and of gaining as many bonus marks as possible. A horse like this will be in a very strong position when it comes to the final test of Show Jumping. The third and last day of the Three-day Event is by no means a high jumping competition. It is simply to demonstrate that after a day of tremendous effort the horse still is capable of jumping a course of show fences. He is bound to be stiff in his limbs, but he must negotiate with precision some twelve obstacles in the arena or lose ten marks for every mistake he makes. It is surprising how great an influence on the result one fallen pole may have on the competition. In fact, the Show Jumping Phase, despite the comparatively easy fences, is not to be dismissed lightly.

It should be appreciated that it is useless to concentrate on training one's horse simply for cross country work. Most competitors enjoy this phase above all others, but if one wishes really to excel in Trials one must be ready to spend the time on preparation for every single phase of the Event.

The first step in my own training programme always has been the dressage. Naturally, I have known beforehand that the horse is able to jump, but when actually I decide to start training a horse for Trials I forget the jumping side and concentrate solely on dressage until I have gained a considerable measure of obedience to the aids. My first aim is to get the horse going quietly and confidently in all paces. He must learn to walk, trot and canter correctly, to develop rhythm through these good basic paces and move from one pace to the other fluidly and without effort. The work at the walk and trot alone generally takes weeks, but it is worth spending time in these early stages. Once the horse achieves steady and correct basic paces he will have little difficulty in absorbing any of the later work, so I practise transitions from walk to trot on circles and straight lines and then gradually extend the range of my demands. The horse learns to bend correctly on the circle and in corners, his whole body curved to the circle or corner line, and then to adapt this length bend in changes of direction. He learns to move in a straight line at all paces—much more difficult than one imagines—and to keep his head steady even during the transitions from pace to pace. As the training progresses the horse will learn the work on two tracks so that in the final Three-day Dressage Test the movement of counter change of hand on two tracks presents no difficulty to him. I teach my horses to move sideways, yield to my leg, comparatively early in training. I find it of inestimable value for correcting quarters which insist on swinging to the side. Once the horse has learnt to yield to the leg he will straighten out immediately to pressure on the offending side, and it is an aid the horse accepts quite readily. The quarters are most apt to swing at the canter, but this aid makes it comparatively easy to correct. The canter should be practised firstly on circles as this is easier for the horse, and then on straight lines. If he is confused as to whether he should be leading with one leg or another, work on the circle soon dispels this. It is natural for the horse to lead with his inside fore leg on the circle, so one uses this to teach him the aids to canter right or left.

Once he has achieved the required standard in this initial schooling one can commence work over cavalletti. These are poles fixed at regular intervals six inches above the ground so that the horse trots over them one pace to one pole at a time. It is a valuable balancing and suppling exercise and encourages the horse to pay attention to the line of obstacles. The next stage is to trot over small fences, perhaps with poles on the approach ground to ensure the horse reaches the fence balanced and ready for the perfect take off. The trainer must do all in his power to develop his horse's bascule, so that in negotiating any obstacle the horse's line of flight describes a perfect arc from take off to landing. These early exercises are invaluable in developing the bascule. Once the horse jumps small fences and combinations with ease he is ready to approach them from various angles, so that in competitions he will be able to save valuable seconds. Progress from here is obvious, and one begins to jump larger fences and to face natural obstacles either out hunting or in cold blood as preparation for the cross country. Finally comes the last concentrated effort for a Three-day Event. One assumes one's horse has been trained systematically in his dressage, can jump with courage most cross country fences and is able to negotiate a course of show jumps with few or no mistakes.

The main problem in a Three-day Event is that the horse is to face a very severe test. He must be supremely fit, and this means he must follow a training programme which ensures his arriving for the Event at the peak of his form. Some horses become fit more easily and with less work then others, but generally I have found that a ten-week final training period is the answer. At the start of these ten weeks my horses have been either in ordinary work or simply out every day for schooling. I begin each day with dressage work and follow this up with road work starting with half an hour and gradually increasing to two hours per day. Thus the horse's legs are hardened by a gradual process, and each part of the training programme is carried out to guard against subjecting the horse to the sudden strain which spells the disaster of a break down. In the sixth week of the period I begin to include some galloping work, but, again, it is a gradual process and starts with a mere half mile canter. The eventual aim is to complete a two and a half mile stretch at three-quarter speed and be able to pull up with a horse completely unconcerned. The only galloping done at full speed is over short, sharp stretches. At the end of these ten weeks the horse should be supremely fit. His dressage work has been progressing week by week and he should be capable of gaining an average of seven out of ten marks throughout the dressage test. This will place him well up with the leaders. His jumping training also has not been neglected, for cross country practice is included easily in the road work, and special time afforded for the show jumping. His preparation has been aided further by careful planning of diet and strict adherence to the timetable no matter how uncomfortable this may have proved to rider or groom! The result of such a programme is bound to be that the horse starts the competition with a very good chance of success. Always there is the unexpected, and one needs desperately the presence of good luck throughout the three days. The latter, however, is not to be bought, and for the few who are determined in their efforts to succeed there is no alternative but to resign themselves to hard work. The weeks of training pass slowly, and with adverse conditions it becomes a feat of will power to adhere faithfully to the programme. Only the truly dedicated will complete it fully and, undoubtedly, it will be their efforts which are rewarded. Sometimes fate is unkind, and a slip or unwarranted fall puts paid completely to the hopes of a competitor who perhaps deserves better luck, for he has done all in his power to bring himself and his horse to the peak of fitness. This, however, is much more likely to happen to the ill-prepared or unfit horse, and one cannot be persuaded that the systematic training programme is anything but sheer necessity.

Fortune, for the most part, consistently favours the brave. Take courage, then, and train properly to meet the trials of the Three-day Event.

THE PERFECT GOOD HORSE

To have the Head and Legs of a Stag, the Ears and Tail of a Fox, the Neck of a Swan, the Breast of a Lyon, the Buttocks of a Woman, and the Feet of an Ass.
"THE COMPLEAT JOCKEY", 17TH CENTURY

A staunch supporter of the 3 Day Event: Mr. J. R. Hindley riding Speculation

Hazards of all sorts at Harewood: Miss P. Sutcliffe on Winterset

"... *three pairs of heels in the air together*"
From a drawing "The Kadir Cup, 1924" by Lionel Edwards

158

Carclew's First Kadir Cup

BRIGADIER J. SCOTT COCKBURN, D.S.O., M.C.

TO WIN the Kadir Cup had been my ambition since I started pig-sticking and had first experienced the thrill of a top-speed gallop through breast-high grass and scrub, a strong boar in front of me and fellow sportsmen racing for the "spear" at my side. The winning of the Kadir Cup for the first time gave me, perhaps, the biggest thrill of my life. On the other two occasions when I again won it I had the satisfaction of creating records and, although the excitement of the competition was still there, the big thrill of achievement was missing.

It was in 1924 that I first won. Two years before I had been in the final heat with one other competitor against me, Pat Baldwin, of the 12th Cavalry, on Blue Barron. It was the year H.R.H. the Prince of Wales was present at the meeting and when he won the Hoghunters' Cup, a four mile point-to-point, on Bombay Duck. In the final of that year my horse, Cherry Blossom, when leading, fell in a blind nullah and broke a hind leg, thus knocking us out and giving a walk-over to Pat. It was a cruel blow to me. Cherry Blossom was my first real pig-sticker, a horse that had learned the game from A to Z at Muttra. Handy as a polo pony, very fast, and as staunch as a rock. It seemed that he was almost impossible to replace . . . until I got Carclew. I shall never be able to decide which was the better. Both Indian stud bred horses, Cherry Blossom was up to more weight and possibly would stay longer; maybe he lacked a little of Carclew's fire. Carclew won all his heats by his dash, and was only beaten when over 20 years old, and then twice in long tiring hunts and giving 2 stones to his competitors. When I left India I took him to England with me, where he died at the ripe old age of thirty-two.

The entries were well up to average and, as usual, competitors were drawn in heats on the evening preceding the first day's hunting. There were four previous winners of the Kadir at the meeting, Marsh of the I.C.S., Paynter, West and Bates, all of the Gunners. I was to draw one of them in my heats; two of the others reached the semi-finals.

In my first heat I was drawn against Yorke on Solomon, well named, a wise old pig hunter making up in training what he lacked in speed, and against Vaughan-Hughes, also of the Gunners, on Golden Syrup, a quick, handy and fast little horse. General Wardrop was our umpire and was soon able to slip us on a good boar which was well into his stride before we started. Carclew got on terms almost at once, but perhaps I hurried things too much, for the boar, rattled by the pace, put a foot in a hole and turned a somersault. I speared him in the belly as I passed and pulled up to show my spear to the umpire. General Wardrop examined the spear and, to my horror, said, "I'm sorry, but you can't show blood." True enough there was no blood on the spear. By wounding in the belly there was nothing to show but a smear of fat!

My feelings are better imagined than described. I had wasted valuable seconds in pulling up and the others were a quarter of a mile ahead! You do not need luck to win the Kadir, but no one can stand up against bad luck. There was nothing to be done but go all out to catch up, and this I did with all speed, Carclew seeming as eager to get into the hunt again as I. Yorke had been making the running in my absence; Vaughan-Hughes was newer to the game, though I think he had the faster horse. On getting level Carclew got in on a sharp jink, and this time, making no mistake, we stayed on the boar's tail and took the first opportunity of a heavy spear. It was the most agonising heat I ever rode!

In the next round I was drawn against a previous winner of the Kadir, Colin West on his Mustapha and "John Willie" Mansell on Pirate. Both, especially the former, had done a lot of hunting with the Meerut Tent Club and both I felt were dangerous. As it turned out, one, I never knew which, proved to be even more dangerous than I had anticipated. "Chink" Phipps was our umpire this time. There had been a long delay in getting off heats, and umpires, in order not to hold up the competition, were slipping competitors on pig that, to say the least, would not have passed for height or for weight the standards of an ordinary tent club. My one nightmare in the Kadir has always been to be slipped on an undersized pig. With a rideable boar you know where you are. He is the animal that you and your horse are accustomed to hunt. Instinctively you know what he is likely to do under all circumstances, when he is going to jink, when he is going to squat, double back or charge.

With a small pig it is quite different. He is not an angry warrior leading you through all the hazards of the jungle in an attempt to shake you off and ready, should these tactics fail, to turn and rend you. He is a frightened animal frantically trying to dodge his pursuers and dodging them with turns so sharp that the best of horses cannot follow. With the one a good horse can stay, taking jink for jink, keeping on his tail till the time comes to close in and spear. With the other it is often a matter of luck, and the pig may turn back to be speared by the worst member of the heat, following some way behind. But it sometimes happens that it is necessary to slip heats on these smaller pig, and it was one of these that we hunted.

We were all up together, Mustapha in the centre, Pirate on the right and Carclew on the left, the pig travelling at a cracking pace over easy going with the three of us riding a finish behind him. It was a quick hunt. When we closed on the pig our knees were almost touching; then, to my horror, the pig jinked right and sharp back. To swing round with the others would have put me on the outside of a circle and with valuable distance lost. There was nothing to be done but turn left about and trust to Carclew coming round before the others. This is a big test on a horse accustomed to hunt pig, as did Carclew, like a greyhound a hare. However, he pulled up in a couple of lengths, then round on his hocks and away again in his stride. The turn had actually given me an advantage, for I was up on the pig just before the others and speared. Remembering the awful moments of my previous heat when I had speared and could not show blood, this time I speared, pulled up and pinned the pig to the ground. And this was the moment when my competitors proved so dangerous. One of them, riding with his spear down or held across his horse's withers, ran the point seven inches into Carclew's dock. I thought he was done. Blood spouted out, and I felt I would have lost that heat a thousand times rather than lose so gallant a horse. It was with a heavy heart that I led him back the five or six miles that separated us from the camp.

Carclew was still bleeding when I got him home to the horse lines, and I had quite made up my mind that I would have to scratch him, since further participation in the competition seemed out of the question. I have always blamed myself for getting a horse cut by boar, but accidents such as the death of Cherry Blossom two years before and now this chance spear wound in Carclew seemed a cruel turn of misfortune. Captain Thomas, of the Royal Army Veterinary Corps, however, who had kindly come to look after the horse casualties at the meeting, took a more optimistic view. He told me that if nothing vital had been punctured, it might be just possible to run the horse the following day.

Carclew's First Kadir Cup

To ascertain the damage it was necessary to probe the wound; any attempts to do so were strongly resented by Carclew, who stood up on end and refused anyone to come near him. Three times we tried to throw him, and three times he stood up on end and came over backwards. The bleeding started afresh, and my heart was in my mouth whenever he was approached. I was in favour of giving him best, for sending him into Meerut in a horse box and for performing an operation in the hospital there. However, Thomas persevered and, at the fourth attempt, threw him and we held him down. Thanks to his skill he was able to make a thorough examination of the wound and to close it with three stitches. We sat up most of that night with the horse, coaxing him to feed now and then, but it was not until the early hours of the morning that he became less restless and settled down. I think I had perhaps two hours' sleep and was again at the horse lines at daybreak with Thomas for a final examination. He told me it would be all right to run the horse and that, although there was still some bleeding, of course, he could not be expected to show his best form—I would be doing him no harm. Accordingly, I allowed my entry to stand as it had been drawn, in my semi-final heat. The official account of the heat is as follows:

> "Second heat: Mr. Mansell (R.H.A.), Chief; Captain Scott Cockburn, Carclew (spear); Mr. Freer, Gay Lad. Umpire, Major Yorke.
> "Heat slipped on a moderate pig going forward from the right of line. The three spears got away dead level, and in a fast run-up Scott Cockburn had the advantage. Mansell rode the pig for 50 yards, but Scott Cockburn got it on the first jink and from then onwards did all the work, taking the pig jink for jink, and speared well."

This brings us down to the finals; the next heat was to decide the winner of the Kadir of 1924. The betting was, I think, in favour of Jerry Hugo's Jazz. He was a big, upstanding horse, in the pink of condition, and had won several steeple chases upcountry. Carclew, on the other hand, stood at least a hand shorter and, although fit as could be, was no doubt suffering from his wound and had not yet proved himself in public. For myself I felt as happy as one can be on such occasions, and could not forget how near the Cup had been to my hand only two years ago. However, barring falls or a long run up to the pig in light country when the odds would be on the big-striding horse, it seemed to me that Carclew would more than hold his own. In my opinion, the disadvantages of a big horse out pig-sticking outweigh the advantages. In light country with a long run-up, the big horse will get there first. But when the boar begins to twist and turn or the going is trappy, the smaller horse that is well balanced has that fifth leg which not only gets him over the obstacles which so often appear closely one after the other. It was such, indeed, that proved the undoing of Jazz.

After the semi-final had been contested a halt was called to rest the horses before the final run. The long line of 200 beaters stopped and spectators, sitting on the forty elephants that followed the beaters, discussed the prospects of the two remaining competitors. Jazz did not appear to be any the worse for his long time on the line in his semi-final heat, and Carclew, after a mouth wash and a rub down, was ready to take his part.

As we rode out to take our place in the centre of the line of beaters, General Wardrop, our umpire, examined our spears to ascertain that they were free from any traces of the blood of previous pig. When all was ready Babu, the shikari, mounted on his camel, gave the signal and the parallel lines of coolies and elephants started to move forward. There was no noise except the swish of the high grasses, and a subdued murmur of conversation from the spectators on the elephants. Of what Jerry Hugo was thinking I do not know; none of us uttered a word. I felt that Carclew would win, barring accidents, and I prayed for a good start and a hunt in thick country. I also prayed that we would find a warrantable boar quickly. Every minute spent on the line was tiring to Carclew.

On, on went the beat with now and then a whistle from Babu as he swung the coolies to right or left. A rustle in the grass and sounds of a scurry forward sent our hearts beating as a sow or young pig were put out of their resting-places. After a time the country ahead appeared to be getting lighter, and I hoped that this would not be the time when a good boar broke. At this juncture frenzied shouts from the spectators, who from their elephants could see further ahead than we, indicated that rideable pig was moving on. Nothing was as I would have wished it, for it seemed to be a case of a long run up and light country in which to hunt. General Wardrop trotted with us quietly forward. It seemed that he of all those present was the only one to control his excitement. At last we saw the boar, a big fellow, cantering steadily forward and were given the order to ride.

Carclew, as usual, was away first, but there were over 400 yards to make up before we came on terms with the pig. Jazz was soon level, and I felt that I had got to ride all I knew to keep him there and get the better of him on the turns. A boar of his size in country like that over which we were riding should have been bacon in a few minutes; but, as things happened, maybe watching each other more than the boar, we overrode him. Jerry cast to the left and I to the right, each hoping to pick up the boar and get a start on the other; such a start spelled victory for one of us, for it could never have been caught up. General Wardrop, in his account, of the heat, wrote: "Slipped over easy grass country after a big pig; overrode and lost him inexcusably."

Carclew's First Kadir Cup

No doubt we did, but I was not sorry, wanting as I did to ride in thick country, where the horses would really have to hunt.

It was an anti-climax. I am sure the spectators felt we had wasted a good boar, and that the heat might go on for hours until we should find such another. We rode back to the line with our umpire, and soon the beat had started again with ourselves in the centre. This time we had not long to wait, and it was again the spectators who spotted the boar, another big fellow who broke through the elephants and made off in the direction from which we had been beating. All halted while our umpire led us back through coolies and elephants in the direction which the boar had been seen to take. Jerry Hugo and I afterwards admitted to each other our impatience at this moment.

We felt that General Wardrop was taking things too easily, that he did not seem to mind whether he slipped us or not, that another good boar would be wasted, and this time by him. It was, however, an example of good umpiring. A good umpire never allows his heat to get flustered, he keeps them well in hand, leads them at a slow and steady pace, and uses his pigcraft rather than speed to pick up the line of the boar. Such indeed did General Wardrop on this and also on all occasions when I have had the good fortune to have him umpire my heats. We soon viewed the boar, which had not been hurried by the noise of unnecessary galloping, and were slipped at a trot when riding level and some 300 yards from our quarry.

I can never forget that shouted order, "Ride!" Away went our horses in their stride at once, the boar shooting forward at an increased pace as he heard us. Forgotten was everything else in the world as we each gripped our spears and closed our legs on the good horses under us. Of what happened in the hunt I have but little knowledge. Carclew was up first, and I remember once seeing Jazz by my left knee as he challenged us for first place on the boar's tail. I can remember no incidents but two sharp jinks, which Carclew seemed to anticipate, and the moment when, realising it was the opportunity to close, I embedded my spear up to the shaft in the boar. Actually I had had most of the hunt to myself, for Jazz, galloping all out to pass us, put a foot in a porcupine earth and over he went, a real crumpler with three pairs of heels in, the air together.

Others came up and the boar was killed. Carclew, as he always did at the end of a hunt, bent down and touched the dead boar with his nose, seemingly his silent tribute to a worthy foe. I slackened his girths and led him back, my heart too full to utter, elated at achieving the ambition of all hog hunters and with more than a thought for my gallant Cherry Blossom, who, lying now at rest in his Kadir grave, had carried me so near to victory only two years before.

It is Never too Late

Even for Advanced Dressage

MRS. V. D. S. WILLIAMS

HAVING BEEN BORN into an atmosphere of horses, it is little wonder I spent most of my time as a youngster in the stables. In fact it was my parents' only handle to guarantee my good behaviour.

I graduated into the hunting field at a very early age and revelled in every moment of it. In fact I felt life would indeed be empty without the joy of a beautiful horse beneath me and the excitement of a pack of hounds in full cry in front. Luckily I was to enjoy many good hunts with many good packs for many years. But World War II came along, and I was doomed to other duties which were more arduous and certainly not so pleasant.

As always, even the worst crisis comes to an end sometime, so in 1946 I found myself demobbed and comfortably settled in the South of England with no horse and, furthermore, not having been on one for six years. This dreadful state of affairs had to be rectified.

This was not difficult as my husband was just as mad about horses as I. Luckily for me he was more educated in the Art of Riding, so was a great help and encouragement to me and, in fact, set me well and truly on the road to many happy hours and years of study and work, which included many disappointments and, later, many triumphs.

All this goes to show it is never too late to learn. I can remember as a youngster, whilst in the process of trying to back and school a young horse, saying to myself: "I wish I knew what to do." Alas! In those days there was nobody to teach me, my only instructor being the old family groom whose knowledge was indeed limited. My pathetic efforts consisted of getting up on top, galloping and jumping. If my horses did both of these satisfactorily, I was well and truly happy and neither expected, nor wanted, anything more.

What colossal ignorance! All the same I did have fun out hunting.

I suppose one can say that, owing to not having ridden during World War II, I had lost to a certain degree the desire to go scampering across country and was ready to look for other activities in the horse world; therefore it was not difficult for me to turn to dressage in earnest. Be that as it may, this is exactly what I did.

My first dressage horse was called Pilgrim. He was nine years old when I bought him and was rather dipped in the back, which did not make his work easy. But he was beautiful and kind and gentle, though to the end he found some of the High School movements difficult to perform.

So we set off together to learn the Art of Riding. It was enormous fun. Then we had a wonderful piece of luck which transformed the whole of my riding career.

The year after the Olympic Games were held in London Colonel Podhajsky, Chief of the Spanish Riding School of Vienna, brought his whole Quadrille of horses and riders to England to give a display at the International Horse Show held at the White City. It was the most wonderful spectacle and, needless to say, thrilled me to the core, set my imagination on fire and made me determined to model myself on this brilliant master of the Art of Riding.

He stayed in our house for two weeks, and during this time he gave me several rides on his horse and let me into, what was then for me, the most exciting secrets of teaching a horse obedience to the "aids". This was a big thrill in my life and proved to be of immense value. At last I had got a feel of what I was trying to achieve. At last I knew what I was looking for, and the successes which later came my way were entirely due to Colonel Podhajsky's patient, classical and brilliant teaching.

This was in 1949, and I was well passed middle age when Pilgrim and I started learning the "aids" together. We had lots of fun, made lots of mistakes, but we worked hard and gradually laid the foundation of that bond of harmony and sympathy which must exist between horse and rider. Without this wonderful close association it is difficult to rise to any great heights. There must be total confidence on both sides together with a love of purity, a sense of rhythm, a lot of patience and a great determination to succeed.

Gradually we found the meaning of cadence, and one day the old horse was as thrilled as I to find we could go from one wonderful trot rhythm to an equally good canter rhythm and back again at will. This is pure beauty of movement and has to be felt to be enjoyed. There is much work, though,

It is Never too Late

before this is achieved. Lots of heartaches, lots of disappointments before this elegance and grace of movement is produced and maintained.

It is so important for the rider to know his horse and for him to know and trust his rider. When things go wrong he should say: "What have I done wrong?" and think how he can explain himself better to his horse. Perhaps the "aids" were not quite correct or, maybe, they were not quite clear. It is not right to blame the horse because he does not understand. The rider must make certain he does understand, and only then can he be firm and insist upon obedience. This friendship and trust must continue between horse and rider, when, as I was to find, my horse gave willingly and proudly to my bidding and, in fact, enjoyed every moment we spent together.

The passage is a very high cadenced trot where the horse holds the suspension between the two diagonal beats for a fraction longer than in the ordinary trot. The piaffé is the same high cadenced trot as the passage but it is performed on the spot without any forward movement. Both are difficult exercises, particularly so for Pilgrim, who, as I have already said, was dipped in the back so his back muscles were never really strong enough for these very exacting exercises.

Just as athletes have to perform exercises to enable them to run, jump or swim, so must horses perform exercises every day to strengthen the muscles they must use in order to perform the High School movements. In fact not only High School movements, that comes afterwards, they must be taught to use the correct muscles at the beginning of their work for trotting, cantering and lateral work so that the muscles on one side become as soft and flexible as those on the other side. Only then can the horse become straight and supple and one that is completely obedient and can perform with ease and willingness any exercise asked of him.

One day I was talking to a trainer of elephants who told me that one act had taken two years to perfect. "Because," she said, "we had to get the elephant's muscles strong enough for him to carry all his weight on one leg." A clear lesson on the importance of physical training. Also, I am told our Olympic runners spend the winter months learning ballet dancing!

After ten years of trial and error Pilgrim and I were deemed good enough to be given the honour of being the first British horse and rider to take part in the Grand Prix de Dressage in an Olympic Games. So, with many misgivings, we set sail for Stockholm in 1956 where, if we did not shine, at least we did not disgrace ourselves.

One might say ten years is a long time in which to train a horse. So it is, but it must be remembered that my horse and I were both learning at the same time and our instructor had long since sailed away to a far country. I am stressing this point as an encouragement to others who have to work a lot on their own that it can be done, provided every opportunity is taken to watch the experts and take heed of lessons learnt.

By now I had ridden many horses, trained quite a number up to medium and one other up to Grand Prix standard, had competed abroad with moderate success, watched many fine continental riders working and gained much experience and knowledge. It is astonishing what can be learnt by watching top class classical riders in action. Even now I find new thoughts coming to me whilst studying these people.

I was now ready for my most brilliant of all horses, and here I was very lucky. It is seldom in this life one finds the exact object one is looking for at a critical moment, especially when that object is a horse, but that is just what happened to me.

It was the year after the Games at Stockholm and a little over three years before the Olympic Games which were going to be held in Rome in 1960. I wanted very much to go and compete, but knew my dear old Pilgrim, who was now twenty, was beginning to lose his liberty of action and that I must get another horse quickly, as three years is a very short time in which to train one up to Olympic standard.

Fortune favoured me as I heard about a horse called Little Model with odd breeding. He was by the TB stallion Little Heaven out of a Connemara pony mare, stood barely 15·1 hh, a grey with the most adorable head. Of course I fell in love with him at once and took him home in high ecstasy building, *en route*, wonderful castles in the air, some of which were to come to fruition.

I wanted very much to take him to Rome but knew a lot of hard and skilful work was ahead of me, as there was so little time in which to prepare him. I decided to adhere to the old adage of "Make haste slowly" and not try to rush him. Possibly this was the reason of my success, as Little Model quickly grew to have great confidence in me and seemed to enjoy work and giving of his best.

I find it exciting and stimulating starting work on a new horse, and this one had to be good. For six months I concentrated on the trot and canter. I am sure this is important because it is the basis of all training. The horse must be able to go forward in the trot, increase and decrease the pace without losing his rhythm by lengthening and shortening his pace. He must be able to do this at the canter too, and, in my humble opinion, it is the perfecting of this basic training that is the secret of success. If this part of the horse's training is hurried, the rider falls into traps that only become apparent later when they are more difficult to correct. If the horse gets bored with too much or too concentrated work, he thinks out all sorts of evasions to stop this irritation, when his progress is halted, because the trainer must go back in his work in order to eliminate these evasions which have been provoked by hurried or sloppy work and should never have been allowed to appear.

Again I must stress the importance of knowing one's horse. Some horses like work and can be kept at it longer, on the other hand, others hate it and seem to take pleasure in rebelling. These are difficult horses and must be treated with great care and not forced in any way. In all cases it is the classical rider who knows exactly how much to give his horse and when to stop. Generally speaking I find three-quarters of an hour is enough work, I then take my horse out for a jolly or a walk in the country. All the same, lessons must be learnt, and it is necessary to continue with an exercise until it is correct when the horse can be rewarded by a pat and work stopped. In this way he gets to know that he gets a rest when he is obedient.

So, Little Model and I continued our work together. We got the trot and canter rhythm good, and, all this time having done bending exercises, he became both straight and supple. We progressed with lateral work, pirouettes and changes in the air when, horror he went lame! It proved to be a splint so we blistered him at once, which turned out to be a pure waste of time as he had then to be fired before he finally became sound. As can be imagined, I was sure this had put paid to any chance of my getting to Rome, especially as this happened to be that very hard summer when we had no rain for months and the ground was as hard as iron when I started work again, and Little Model was not allowed out of the indoor riding school until the rain came towards the end of the summer. However, such was his capacity for concentration and work he improved quickly and took a delight in learning new lessons. It was as if he were just as determined as I to go to the Olympic Games. As if driven by some inner force he tried his best to perform these intricate exercises and we made great strides forward. Everything appeared to be easy for him, which I am quite sure was due to all the care I had taken with his early training, making sure he knew every degree of my "aids" so there could be no possibility of mistaken meanings, also to his quick brain and superb sense of balance. Mistakes there would be in plenty, but they had painstakingly to be reduced to a minimum.

Some people are under the impresssion that High School movements are artificial and do not like to see horses performing these exercises. This is not so at all. Every movement performed in High School has a purpose and is completely natural. How often has one seen horses "high-tailing" it in the field when they get excited? This is the Passage. Or they gallop off performing miracles of pirouettes when reaching the end of the paddock.

In the olden days horses were taught to fight in combat; hence the Capriole, where they leap into the air and kick out at their foe; or the Courbette, where they stand on their hind-legs in order to protect their riders. All these movements have meaning and all are performed by the horse in his natural state, they are only perfected by the rider and demanded at his will.

The passage, piaffé and change in one time are the most difficult movements for the horse to learn. The latter came fairly easily to Little Model as did the passage, but the piaffé was more difficult.

Some people think the passage should be taught before the piaffé and others vice versa. One often hears, "When the passage is offered it should be taken." This is what I did and, maybe, it was wrong. Here, I think, is a difficulty, as it is not easy until one tries, when it may be too late, to know which to teach first. There is no doubt about it, in some cases, if the passage is taught before the piaffé, the horse will find it difficult to learn the latter. But, on the other hand, it is sometimes the other way round, though I think mostly it is better to teach the piaffé first when the passage should be no problem.

The piaffé can be taught either from "in hand", when the trainer is on his feet and carries a long whip whilst the horse is on rather short side reins. This requires a certain amount of physical strength on the part of the trainer, because the impulsion created by the whip must be directed upwards and not allowed to go forward more than a few inches at a time. When the horse begins to understand he has got to trot with only a slight forward movement, an assistant can be put on top whilst the trainer continues the same work on his feet. Finally he gets on top and the horse should, by then, understand what is required of him, and only time perfects the movement.

The other way is for the trainer to stay in the saddle and get an assistant with a long whip to help create impulsion, while the trainer controls the forward movement. The assistant uses the whip according to the horse's reactions. Sometimes it is enough to just swish it behind the horse, but, generally speaking, a tap on top of the rump is best. I do not like the hocks tapped unless the assistant is very skilled, as it is possible to get the horse lifting one diagonal higher than the other with this method.

I started the first method, but, as I had only a short rein attached to the cavesson with which to control him, I soon found I was not nearly strong enough to hold Little Model and gave it up for the second method. This exercise was the slowest and most difficult for him to learn and, in fact, he had only just got it established in time to go to the Olympic Games in Rome. Even then he kept on improving for many months afterwards.

I am quite sure for a big competition like the Olympic Games or a European Championship the horse should be capable of performing all the Airs and Graces of the High School at least one year before the competition, so that the trainer has plenty of time in which to perfect the movements the horse finds difficulty in performing.

I have tried to put down some of my thoughts and experiences with regard

It is Never too Late

to training horses for High School. The work is fascinating to a degree and immensely satisfying and absorbing. It can fill one's life and be a source of joy, not only to oneself but to all those who love to see the horse performing in all his glory, beauty and grace, proudly giving his best to the bidding of his rider.

There are riders who ruin their horses and there are horses which improve their riders.

ALVISI

" The 'orse and 'ound were made for each other, and natur threw in the fox as a connecting link between the two."

JORROCKS

" There are three things that are never boring to see: a swift swimmer swimming, a young girl dancing, and a young horse running. And three things that are never tiring to speak of: God, and love, and the racing of horses."
TALE OF THE GIPSY HORSE
(*from Destiny Bay*) by
DONN BYRNE

IS THIS THE ANSWER?
"As soon as the horseman knows how to use his legs, it matters very little whether he chooses curb or snaffle, since the action of either on the horse's mouth is in fact of the very slightest."

GUSTAVE LE BON

SCHOOLING YOU AND YOUR HORSE
See that a ride in the open country is just as pleasant for your horse as for yourself. Let him take an interest in the scenery; let him nibble an occasional leaf or tuft of grass which may tempt him . . . distractions which will counteract any primitive desire to return to the stable and the oats!

A golden bit does not make the horse any better.

PROVERB

Everyman's Goal

British Successes in International Riding

PAMELA MACGREGOR-MORRIS

CURRENT BRITISH SUCCESSES in international riding, both collectively as a team and singly as individuals, are more numerous and impressive than they have been at any time during the last ten or twelve years. The early 1950s may well be regarded in retrospect as the heyday of equestrian sport in this country, when Colonel Harry Llewellyn and his contemporaries made frequent forays upon the Continent and returned with the lion's share of the spoils, including the gold medals at the Helsinki Olympic Games.

By 1956, when the Games were held in Stockholm, we had already ceded pride of place to Germany and Italy, and they, with the now powerful squad of gladiators from the United States, were still in the forefront at Rome in 1960. Now, however, we have fought our way back to what should prove to be a position even stronger than that which we held previously.

Our strength lies in the fact that the mantle of supremacy, which formerly fell on a select few, separated by a great gulf of disparity from the run-of-the-mill British rider, has now been stretched to cover perhaps a dozen, each of whom could give a good account of himself in a Nations' Cup. More important still, both they and their horses have youth on their side and are able to give some twenty years to many of those who shone most brightly in the last decade.

The resurgence of Britain as a world power in show jumping probably first made itself felt in 1961 when David Broome, who had already won an individual bronze medal on Sunsalve the previous year, won the Men's

European Championship at Aachen on the same horse. Then, in 1962, David Barker and Mister Softee won the title for Britain for the second successive year, and after the English show season finished went on the North American circuit, where they covered themselves with glory.

Nor were the lady riders hiding their lights, but this was nothing new, for Pat Smythe's colours have never yet been lowered for long and British ladies have seldom been beaten by foreign ones. Indeed, since its inception in 1957 the Ladies' European Championship has only once gone out of this country. Pat Smythe has won it four times and three times in succession, completing her hat trick in 1963 on Flanagan.

By the middle of the 1962 season Britain's future prospects for a world-class Nations' Cup team were already beginning to look very bright. In addition to David Barker and David Broome, Harvey Smith had hit the headlines with O'Malley, the Canadian-bred horse which he took over in July and on whom later that month he won the valuable John Player Trophy at the White City. Peter Robeson's Firecrest, after a long and meticulous preparation, had come into his own as a Cup horse, and so had the spectacular newcomer Merely-a-Monarch, for which both the Italians and the Americans had offered very large sums of money. Britain's victory, in late August, in the Nations' Cup in Rotterdam signalled the beginning of a new era in the annals of British show jumping, and events in 1963 proved beyond a doubt that this was no flash in the pan.

During this season four Nations' Cups came home to Britain, the first from Rome, which has always taken a lot of winning. Among the vanquished were both the home team and the Germans, the two crack European contingents. Two months later, British riders won the coveted Prince of Wales' Cup at the White City for the first time in six years, and the writing on the wall was legible to the world. Once again we were able to engage and defeat the best.

Before the war, British successes in the realm of equestrian sport were largely confined to those of the Army teams, competing against other cavalry officers at home and abroad. At the International Horse Show at Olympia certain civilians made their mark in individual competitions, but selection for a British team was confined to serving officers. Thus to ride for one's country was exclusively a military ambition.

Today all that has changed. Since mechanisation of the Army opened the British team to civilian riders the inclusion of a soldier has become the exception rather than the rule. The first non-military team went abroad to Nice and Rome in 1947, and once the precedent became established the show jumping fraternity multiplied exceedingly. Although on the professional level there is less desire for international recognition—and professional riders are in any case debarred from participation in the Olympic Games and several *grand prix* events—the show jumping ladies and many of the younger men, the bulk of them farmers' sons who can combine their riding with their livelihood without serious detriment to either, hold team aspirations very near to their hearts.

There are still, of course, a great many people who ride simply and solely for their own amusement rather than for that of the general public. Most of those who hunt have little or no desire to appear before the world at large in mid-summer disporting themselves over artificial fences in the show ring. Though a small proportion of them have gravitated to the exclusively amateur sport of combined training, the successes of our show jumping team may be said to have left hunting people virtually unmoved.

But the victories of the British team, and particularly that of Colonel Harry Llewellyn, Colonel Duggie Stewart and Wilf White in the 1952 Olympic Games at Helsinki, did make a tremendous impact on a large section of the riding public.

In the 1930s this public was divided, like Caesar's Gaul, into three parts; the gentry, the military and the farmers. The suburban horseman hardly existed, and riding schools and livery stables, unless they were in a hunting area, had a hard time in making ends meet. During the last twenty years, there has arisen a fourth dimension of the horse world, and one that by sheer weight of numbers is probably now as influential as the other three put together. It may well prove to be the saviour of the horse world as a whole and it is undoubtedly very strongly influenced by British successes in international show jumping.

This new dimension of riders has sprung up in what might hitherto have been regarded as apparently unlikely places—in the industrial cities and their environs, and in the subtopian commuter belt a little further removed from the metropolis. If one classifies the British public in only two categories, these are townspeople. They ride at weekends, or on summer evenings on their return from work. They have turned to horses from their offices and factories. Few of them will ever own a horse, but they derive enormous pleasure from riding hirelings and they are responsible for the tremendously increased interest in riding *per se*.

Whereas the majority of country people ride in order to hunt, the townsman rides for the sake of riding. Indeed, he is often quite apathetic towards hunting. To "go for a ride" is, for him, an end in itself, though the more ambitious are able, once they have achieved a modicum of security in the saddle, to set their sights higher to the level of competitive riding with others of similar backgrounds and capabilities. Elementary dressage, show jumping and horse trials are all available to him at his own level of performance under

Everyman's Goal

the auspices of the recently formed association of British riding clubs, which have become to the adult novice rider what the Pony Club has been to the young entry for over thirty years.

Just how much are these weekend riders influenced by the successes of our international teams? Consciously, perhaps, not at all, but subconsciously the existence of someone like Pat Smythe must make a considerable impression as a model to be emulated. Her emergence, some fifteen years ago, as a national figure has continued to make an impact, particularly in view of her self-acknowledged lack of material advantages. If she could reach the dizzy heights of international supremacy with sheer determination and ability, a lot of young women must have reasoned that they could do the same.

Even now, the proportion of the young girls to young men in the show ring is very high, and if none of them has yet succeeded in carving for herself a niche in the Smythe category, they have most of them enjoyed their moments of triumph to encourage them and spur them on to greater efforts.

Show jumping, even for those with unlimited financial resources, must always be a struggle. It is a tough sport in more ways than one. The apprenticeship is long and hard, disappointments are a commonplace, luck plays an almost unfairly disproportionate part, and even in the top echelons of the sport the pursuit of victory involves its acolytes in long, uncomfortable journeys, irregular hours, and exposure to the vagaries of the British climate. The expenses are high, and even with the benefits of sponsorship there are scant financial emoluments to allay the dubious pleasures of spending six months of the year with a travelling horse box as the nerve centre of existence.

Though a rider cannot have one without the other, on the international plane the level is appreciably higher. Travelling, often by air, is comparatively comfortable, visiting teams are usually accommodated in the best hotels and fed on a similar scale, with a car and driver provided and post-show entertainments and hospitality offered nightly. But ninety per cent of the show jumpers never escape from the treadmill of the national shows, even for a brief few days at a Continental C.H.I. or unofficial international show. They must sustain themselves in the belief that it is better to journey hopefully than to arrive.

The influence of British equestrian successes is probably more strongly felt among the thousands of children who belong to the Pony Club than it is anywhere else. Membership of this admirable institution increases every year, and these young people, of an age when hero-worship is an essential emotion, are definitely inspired by idols such as David Broome and David Barker—particularly as so many of the younger international riders were themselves active in the Pony Club until comparatively recently. Then the overwhelming success of the British Junior team, only once beaten in eight years in the European Championship, has provided a terrific stimulus to the young.

Anneli Drummond-Hay provides a shining example of what can be achieved by the combination of natural talent allied to hard work and the will to win. Having taken the combined training world by storm with victories in the three-day events at Burghley and Badminton on Merely-a-Monarch, she then set out with the same horse to excel in the more demanding and specialised sport of show jumping. A year later she was a member of the first British team to go abroad that season, and having covered herself with glory at Rome comes into the category of an Olympic possibility. It is a success story beyond most adults' wildest dreams, but to the young, imbued with the blessing of imagination, it is entirely feasible and provides a splendid spur to their own equestrian activities and ambitions.

The autograph-hunters of today, who will mob anyone wearing a red coat on a showground, are the international riders of tomorrow. Although there is a certain annual wastage, particularly among boys, as the Pony Club children leave school and are faced with the necessity for making their way in the world by means other than hippocratic, their love of riding dies hard. Many of them manage to keep in touch with horses through their local riding club, while others spend their summer Saturdays at horse shows.

There can be no doubt that television has proved to be a tremendous asset to the cause of the horse, and especially so among the unconverted. Show jumping has become one of the most popular of all televised sports and has been responsible for arousing a feeling for the horse among those who have never before got closer to one of them than an annual modest investment on the Derby or an office sweepstake on the Grand National. Some of them now spend their holidays at one of the pony trekking centres that have sprung up in recent years all over the British Isles. On the back of a Welsh cob or a Highland pony they explore the wilder countryside, and though they may never go out of a walk they can identify themselves, in their own minds at least, with the d'Inzeos and the Winklers of this world. Their lives have become enriched by a contact, however small, with horses, which stemmed from the night that they clung to the edges of their three-piece suite and watched someone-or-other win the King George V Cup in their own front parlour.

To bring the Royal International Horse Show into every home is not, however, in itself sufficient to maintain an interest in horses generally and to ensure their continued popularity with the public. It is also necessary for British riders to be able to go abroad and win, and to beat the foreigner on his home ground. Chauvinism or the team spirit, call it what one will, is a very necessary ingredient of the interest of the man in the street. To cheer on

Everyman's Goal

the British rider, to become partisan, is vital to complete enjoyment of an international competition. Let the man who pays his half-crown to see the show remain for too long on the losing side and the turnstiles will cease to click. He has no objection to standing to attention for a foreign anthem now and again, but he also wants to see the Union Jack fluttering on the flagpole in its turn.

Fortunately, show jumping in Britain since the war has continued to improve. Horses and their standard of training and performance, riders and their horsemanship, courses and their construction get better year by year. Happily, too, there has never been an entirely lean period in the annals of British show jumping. The pendulum swings, of course, and the team has had its setbacks as well as its triumphs; but even when our record in Nations' Cups has left something to be desired there have always been individual horses and riders to win competitions and lift our reputation as a riding nation out of the ruck.

The present happy state of our international status may be ascribed to a diversity of reasons, and fate has also played its part. The policy of sending more riders abroad, the encouragement of the young by framing special competitions for them, the staging of instructional courses for young riders have all played their part. So too has the foundation of the All England Jumping Course at Hickstead in Sussex, where both horses and riders can gain experience over the only continental-type obstacles in the British Isles, thanks to the good offices of W. D. and H. O. Wills. The increase in sponsorship has also contributed by enabling riders to cover their expenses and perhaps even to end the season on the credit side.

Perhaps the most infallible barometer as to the popularity of any commodity is the relationship between supply and demand. Ten years ago breeders of non-thoroughbred stock both in this country and in Ireland were giving up wholesale. Today there are more horses being bred than at any time since the arrival of the motor car. Many of the Irish farmers who found rearing calves a more lucrative policy than running brood mares and store colts have turned back to horses again. Prices are soaring, and any young horse with any pretension to a jumping potential is hard to come by at any price.

The golden age of the horse, which was hitherto believed to lie in the past, may belong instead to the future. And to Britain's performance in international riding competitions must go the greater part of the credit for this renaissance.

Foxhunting Begins at Forty!

PETER PASQUA

FOUR YEARS AGO, foxhunting was to me something seen once a year on Christmas cards representing an exclusive sport of the landed gentry and their lady admirers, a closed shop unless you were fortunate enough to have been born within their sporting circle, and it certainly never entered my head for a moment that I would ever foxhunt; the nearest I got to it was when looking at old hunting prints I would envy the mounted gentlemen in pink, and think how greatly improved one's chances would be with the young fillies of the day to don such dandy and irresistible clothing. The skill, courage, determination and years of qualifying experience necessary to attain such an exalted position to warrant the splendid clothes never so much passed through my mind. Foxhunting was a world quite apart from mine.

At the age of 40 years I married a girl who had spent most of her life in the hunting field, and it was with complete disbelief that I listened to her explaining how it was indeed possible for me also to ride a horse to hounds. Never having ever ridden a horse before, I could only feel complimented and laugh. She was very persistent that I take to this way of life, a way of life that required a country property, stables and land, horses and staff, horsebox and saddlery, time and funds—an absolute contrast to my existing life in a London apartment which formed the background to a 10 hour day, six days a week, toiling in the family business with, at the most, six weeks ski-ing every year as the reward for my labour.

My wife's proposals would mean a radical change—far easier and more practical, thought I, if she learned to ski. With this object in view I fitted her out with the most glamorous clothes and ski paraphernalia and took her off to St. Moritz, convinced that she would return a ski convert, but it was not to be so; for within 24 hours of arriving she had discovered a school of equitation in St. Moritz, horses raced on ice, ponies pulled sleighs, and it was around these things that her interest developed instead of the all exhilarating pastime of ski-ing. Her conversation was at no time more than a few minutes off horses or some connected subject, and I began to wonder if there was not, after all, some magic in this horse life which had passed me by.

On returning home, defeated in my object, it was necessary to readjust my thinking. My wife introduced me to one or two of her young fox-hunting friends, charming and human folk. There was, I had to admit, a lot to be said for the horsey life, a lot in which to become interested, a life outside the family business and unlike ski-ing, foxhunting provided over six months' sport annually.

Fate, however, settled the whole issue; business reasons necessitated a move out of London to the country. Within three months we were established in an ideal "hunting box" complete with stabling and a 10 acre paddock in Newmarket, Suffolk; not a hunting county like those of the Shires, but my wife was quick to point out, perhaps the best country in which to start to learn the sport of foxhunting.

The plunge had been taken, all that was needed now was a horse. Every week the "Horses for Sale" columns of *Horse and Hound* were scanned meticulously for a "gift horse", but nothing suitable showed up. Tired of seeing an empty yard, we set out for the Leicester Horse Sales. That day there were some very high quality horses under the hammer fetching correspondingly high prices up to three and four times my self-imposed "limit". Over twenty times I had a horse by the tail but my wife made me leave go, and many of these horses were led out just one bid over mine. Then into the ring came a delightful animal, a large bay heavyweight. He trotted up to the auctioneer's rostrum, grabbed the sales register between his teeth and almost made off with it. This seemed a pleasantly spirited horse, and as the bidding passed my limit I missed the cautionary "No more" from my wife—she had apparently slipped away for a minute. Needless to say my impetuosity won the day and this horse was knocked down to me at just double my limit. My heart sank—I had bought a horse off my own inexperienced bat without seeking the advice of the expert. At that moment, the expert returned to my side and remarked, "I wonder who bought that useless elephant?" I felt quite crushed and longed to turn the clock back because I could sense she meant what she said. I broke the news—it was the first time I had seen her angry; her wrath was poured upon me and not even the catalogue description of the horse—"Very sensible sort, up to 15 stone but will carry anyone, perfect family horse, lovely temperament, etc., etc." —would bring her to believe in my judgement that this was the horse for the novice.

My *faux pas* was railed to Newmarket and my wife and I returned home by car arguing the elephant's merits the whole way. It did not take many days to find out that the horse and rider were two of a pair, a very "green" pair—true the horse was a family horse, he would have stood all day with the whole family on board, but ask him to move and it was impossible—he just loved to be a statue. And even when he decided to move, neither horse nor rider thought alike, invariably going their own separate ways!

For the next two months, every morning saw me out at the crack of dawn hacking for two hours, after which time I felt reasonably at home in the saddle even if not secure, and able to propel this unwilling horse from the walk to the trot to the canter. He never gave any trouble, for he was always ready to stop at the slightest invitation. It was obvious that help was going to be needed from somewhere if either was ever going to see a pack of hounds.

Fortunately, about this time I learned that a certain internationally famous horseman was prepared to instruct a limited number of pupils, even beginners, and eagerly I applied for a vacancy on a two-week course. After a 'phone conversation with this gentleman's wife she left me in no doubt that novices from 8 to 80 years would be most welcome. Early one morning in August, we boxed up the horse in our trailer and set off on the 180 mile journey to the riding centre at Todenham on the Warwickshire–Gloucestershire borders. The journey was somewhat of a nightmare, for at every steep hill the car would stall half-way up, necessitating unboxing the horse, walking it to the top of the hill and boxing it there again. Each time the horse was more reluctant than before to re-enter the box, and but for the help of passers-by we would still be on our way today.

Our arduous journey was soon forgotten on arrival at the Riding Centre —everything was so unlike what had been expected. I was over-awed by the magnificent period Cotswold house, located on high ground in a parkland setting with expansive panoramic views over the glorious Warwickshire countryside, and even more over-awed when introduced to the country squire who was to be my instructor for the next two weeks, and to whom for the rest of this narrative I shall refer to as the "Colonel". The horse was immediately taken over by the stud groom, a friendly and very knowledgeable man from whom a wealth of priceless information on horse management was later to be acquired, an education in itself.

The next fortnight was spent with a morning and afternoon session of instruction. The instruction was put over in such a way that after the first

Foxhunting Begins at Forty!

week I had a good theoretical knowledge of the aids to control a horse, but putting it into practice was quite another thing. Allowing for the fact that this horse of mine was unsuitable, as was confirmed by this doyen of the show-jumping world, I found that the Good Lord had not endowed me with the right-shaped legs to perform the aids. My legs must be deformed, for the Colonel assured me the aids were quite simple and surely did he demonstrate accordingly, but I found it impossible to keep my knees pressed into the saddle and at the same time make contact with the horse's flanks with my heels. His horse would carry out every movement he informed me he was about to do, but despite my watching with an eagle eye as one would a magician, there was not the slighest perceivable movement of his hands or legs. No doubt the result of over 50 years in the saddle. After the first few days' instruction I realised how painful riding could be and could never imagine myself being able to endure four or five hours in the saddle out hunting. The raw patches of flesh on the insides of my knees made mockery of all my endeavours. But for the ceaseless encouragement of my wife and all at the Riding Centre, I would have willingly submitted to the growing conclusion that this sport was not for me. With everybody's help I stuck it out and became determined that I would one day ride in a strong and carefree manner, such as was demonstrated daily by the Colonel's wife as she galloped over the paddocks rounding up her dozens of dogs.

Before the fortnight was out, one of the many interesting people of the horse world who were continuously putting in an appearance at the Centre told me of a heavyweight hunter eminently suitable to take a novice hunting, the property of one Army officer posted overseas, at short notice. "Genuine reason for sale" could truly be applied. It had carried its owner fearlessly and safely across Leicestershire for the last two seasons, the lady making the recommendation had also hunted him in the West Country and considered him an exceptional horse. A better schooled horse was necessary and so I made a quick visit to Oakham and saw out at grass this chestnut hunter—a rising 6, by name Mr. Fabulous, and since re-named Kokki, who was to become a very important person in my life. With his shaggy mane and summer belly he resembled a Suffolk Punch. The owner volunteered to bring him up and let me decide finally in a few weeks' time when he would be fit to be ridden. Swayed more by the horse's reputation than his looks, I agreed, and returned to Todenham.

The fortnight of instruction had been a wonderful experience and one of the most enjoyable holidays of my life. Physically I was a bit of a wreck, but mentally greatly inspired and thrilled at all my newly acquired knowledge of horsemanship which was to enable me to start foxhunting that season.

Three weeks later in company with my wife, I went back to Oakham to see Kokki—his vital statistics had much improved; he now looked a very formidable and frightening character, but a magnificent animal. "Much too strong for you", was my wife's verdict, but I liked him and we accepted the owner's offer to demonstrate the horse's prowess. He had an excellent action, was obedient and responded generously to all his rider asked. What impressed me most was his willingness to move—too much willingness I was later to learn. I was invited to try him, my wife advised "No", but my honour was at stake and so I was lifted into the saddle and handed for the first time a double bridle—it was explained to me but there seemed far too many strips of leather to think about. He moved off at a brisk walk and without any invitation broke into a fast trot; after sorting out the reins, the brakes were applied in what I thought to be the correct manner, but he responded by setting off at a fast canter. It was quite terrifying—I shortened the reins and tried pulling him up but it had the reverse effect—he just went faster around the paddock and then made a bee-line for the exit. I visualised myself going for miles with no hope of stopping him, but fortunately his designs were anticipated by the owner and our wives who spread their arms out and caught the reins as I charged through them. With great relief I dismounted, took another look at him and decided to accept the challenge. He was a wonderful horse—another fortnight with the Professor at Todenham would soon put me in the position of being master. We settled the deal and proudly drove him back to Newmarket.

The next day I exercised him. As I rode out down the drive my heart was in my mouth. After yesterday's performance it would be luck if I returned alive. He was quite quiet till we reached the road whereupon he broke into a fast trot—delightful after the last horse, except that I had asked him to walk. As we approached the cross-roads I begged him to slow down, but I might just as well have not been on his back—he carried on at his fast comfortable trot and on reaching the cross-roads turned left sharply and without warning broke into a canter. This was too much—I shortened the reins bringing my hands to within a foot of the bit, stood up in the stirrups crouched forward over his neck and having got my balance, made a determined effort to bring him back, but to my consternation, he flew into a gallop—only a quarter of a mile ahead there was a hairpin bend and we were on the blind side of the road at that. Nothing would halt him and around the corner we went at full speed with me doing the only thing possible—praying hard that no traffic would be coming and that he would slow down. The former prayer was answered, but he never let up. Ahead lay a mile of straight road with a grass verge on one side—I managed to pull him over to the grass and again applied the brakes with all my might but he just went faster than ever. Then I remembered someone saying "sawing" would

Foxhunting Begins at Forty!

always stop a horse—I tried this in desperation but it only hotted him up still more. By this time my legs and arms were lifeless, I was gasping for breath and flopping about all over the place in the saddle, losing and finding my stirrups, and frankly very nervous. Why, oh! why, had I not stuck to ski-ing; when out of control on skis my instructor had always said, "Keep going, the mountain must sooner or later start going uphill again"—only this thought stopped me from baling out—there was half a mile of straight ahead—just as the mountain must start going uphill again, so the energy of this horse must surely decrease over distance. Wishful thinking, for he just galloped on with no sign of easing up. There remained one last hope—towards the end of the road there was a left turn into a cul-de-sac—I must try and turn him into it—if my strength held out. About 30 yards from the turn I sat back in the saddle and applied the aids I had learned at Todenham, and to my utmost relief he slowed down a little and swung into the side road. I tried to keep him on the turn but still at the canter he went straight for a hedge—what to do now—I had never jumped a horse in my life! Bless him, he must have known this for he jammed on the brakes, throwing me forward up his neck till my legs were almost wrapped around his ears. I remember it seemed very high up there. I quickly eased myself back into the saddle as he nonchalantly nibbled away at the hedge, heaving and sweating almost as much as me. When Kokki was ready—I dare not interrupt his snack and risk another altercation—I headed him for home at the walk feeling somewhat crestfallen and fearful of things to come. We reached the stables with no further trouble, by which time some of my confidence had returned. I recounted the terrifying experience to my wife, and she soon made it clear that the horse had only done what in fact I had asked it to do, i.e. "fly". I was learning.

After these escapades, Kokki and I came to an understanding and no more serious difficulties arose, although he continued to register his realisation that I was a novice by such playful antics in the early morning as presenting his hindquarters every time I attempted to put on the bridle which necessitated dragging the wife out of bed to help. Immediately he saw her he would drop his head and accept the bridle like a lamb. On another day, he took me out into the village only to bring me back to the yard against my will no less than five times, much to my embarrassment and the amusement of all the shopkeepers who rushed to their doorways to watch the battle. However, little by little, I was becoming master. The second visit to Todenham provided the final answers, and after a week's instruction, which included some jumping, the Colonel announced I was expected to hunt for the first time the following Monday.

Feeling most self-conscious in my new top hat and hunting coat, we

Foxhunting Begins at Forty!

hacked one mile to the Meet at Tidmington. I shyly surveyed the scene—
horses and riders faultlessly turned out milling around, the hounds eagerly
awaiting the "off", animated conversation everywhere, stirrup cups being
passed round, foot followers out in force, an exciting atmosphere set against
the background of a perfect day, green fields and a country house to remind
us of the hospitality of the local landlord. I trembled at the thought of what
lay ahead, fearful of not being able to stop Kokki, thereby incurring the
wrath of the Master, which I had been warned must be avoided at all costs.
Would he jump, would he kick hounds, would he barge through gates, all
these things made me apprehensive but it was too late to turn back, for I was,
as it were, seated in the car of the Big Dipper already on the move—there
was no alternative but to sit tight and hope for the best.

The Hunt moved off to draw a field of kale; in no time a fox was put up
with the hounds in hot pursuit. The field galloped off—this was "it", away
went Kokki bucking and kicking in all directions showing his well-being
in no uncertain manner. I managed to stay with him apart from momentary
absences out of the saddle, until the first obstacle—a line of wire fencing with
a gate at one end through which most of the hunt went; in my ignorance I
chose to follow the few over a gap in the wire with disastrous consequences
—loose wire caught up with the horse's hind legs, down he went, tumbling
me over his head into the mud. Solicitous cries of "You all right?" from
everybody as they cantered by, a most welcome helping hand from two
gentlemen in pink, and soon I was back in the saddle with my new hunting
kit truly rid of the gloss and glory of the shop, honourably baptised in rich
Warwickshire soil.

Kokki could not wait to catch up—off we set at a great pace across one
field, out of it over a low hedge into another and soon up with the hunt
again, which was queuing to jump through a gap in a rather large hedge.
My turn came—at least I was certain so—at it we went full tilt—a few
strides away a loud authoritative feminine voice interrupted my concentration with, "My turn, please."—I pulled over to make room, up we went
and once again I lay sprawled in the mud. Kokki was looking after me well;
as before, he stood over me with an expression on his face as if to say, to
quote Jorrocks, "Afall's a h'awful thing". The dear fellow made no attempt
to gallop off without me. Aboard again, there was no holding him, which
made matters most difficult as the stirrups were flying in the wind and every
time the foot jabbed forward to catch them, they infuriatingly disappeared.
As luck would have it there was a check one field on, and it was possible to
put myself together again.

"Always follow someone who knows his country," my wife had often
advised. Who better then than the Colonel, who was over in the corner

of the field on his own, standing in his stirrups inspecting the other side of a 6 foot hedge. He came back 20 yards, drove his horse forward at great speed and just flew over with plenty to spare. He seemed to be airborne for an interminable time. Once he was clear, I followed determined to emulate the Professor, but Kokki knew better and braked hard as he breasted the hedge sending me three-quarters the way up his neck—from this point of vantage I could see he was absolutely right—we could never have cleared it together— a yawning 5 foot wide ditch lay menacingly the other side. I never took the liberty of following the Colonel again, and contented myself then with joining the main body of the field who had by this time cut off 3 foot from the hedge where over we popped.

All went well for the next two hours as we moved from cover to cover across fields and through gates. Then there was sudden activity—everybody set off in different directions—the hounds could be seen streaming away on a line in the far distance. For the next hour the hounds ran hard almost non-stop, we rode across field after field, sometimes through gates, sometimes over fences, on and on, would it never end, perspiration poured down my face at times blinding me. Never had I experienced such exhaustion, but the thrill of still being "there" urged me on. Kokki must have realised from my being so loose in the saddle that we would have parted company at every fence had he jumped conventionally, and so he would almost stop at each fence and slowly cat-jump over, which threw me into the air, but somehow he was always there to catch me on part of his neck or body. He would always wait for me to find my way back into the saddle. The fox ultimately went to ground and the Master decided to take his hounds home, much to my relief and great elation—I had stayed with hounds to the end on my first hunt, just how, I will never know. Triumphantly I hacked back; battered body, wrenched arms and bleeding knees in no way detracted from what had been one of the greatest days of my life. How tremendously worthwhile had all the effort been, and what an enormous amount I had yet to learn to enjoy this sport to the full.

* * *

I can now look back on three seasons' hunting; no more do I suffer physically or from horse nonsense, being able now to more or less sit in the saddle correctly and to assert my authority more definitely. Foxhunting and all associated with it has become my reason for living, a new life of pleasure has opened up before me; foxhunting has started to mean more to me than just staying with my horse and the field; the hounds at work now interest me, the horn keeps me informed as to what is going on, the habits of the fox, scenting conditions, all this and more opens up yet other fascinating sides of this great sporting pastime. This new-found enjoyment I owe to my wife, who tirelessly spurred me on; to Colonel J. Talbot-Ponsonby and his wife, Daphne, who gave so much encouragement and placed at my disposal the advantage of their life-time's experience in equitation and the hunting field; to the traditional generosity of M.F.H.s and Hunt members, landowners and farmers and hunt subscribers from all walks of life, who always made me so welcome. My gratitude is also due in no small measure to my very wonderful horse, Kokki, who has become an unending source of pleasure and affection. Together we look forward to many, many more seasons of foxhunting.

FOXHUNTER'S COMPANY
Select is the circle in which I am moving,
Yet open and free the admission to all;
Still, still more select is the company proving,
Weeded out by the funker and thinned by the fall;
Yet here all are equal—no class legislation,
No privilege hinders, no family pride:
In the "image of war" show the pluck of the nation;
Ride, ancient patrician! democracy, ride!

BROMLEY DAVENPORT
THE DREAM OF AN OLD MELTONIAN

An easterly wind and a lowering sky,
A straight-necked fox, with a scent breast high;
I pray for no more, unless a good start
At the tail of my hounds on the horse of my heart.

T. SCOTT ANDERSON

People talk about size, shape, shoulders, quarters, blood, bone, muscle, but for my part give me a hunter with brains, he has to take care of the biggest fool of the two and think for both.

G. J. WHYTE MELVILLE

A cub-hunting morning with the Croome Hunt as the huntsman blows hounds away

Colonel Jack Talbot-Ponsonby leading a group of followers of the North Cotswold hunt near Broadway

Final judging of the heavyweights at Windsor

A strong class of mountain and moorland ponies

Meditations on Judging

COL. G. T. HURRELL, O.B.E.

IT IS A MATTER of considerable concern that through old age and ill health so many of the older judges are fading out and so few young ones coming on to fill their places. With more people now riding for pleasure than ever before, it would seem a simple matter to add to the judges' panels. However, although the committees responsible do their best to find new blood, few names are added to the lists. Junior or learner panels have been tried out with a certain amount of success, but some judges are rather shy to divulge their honest opinions to strange young people, as their remarks are not always treated with the strictest confidence. This can be understood, as most beginner judges are rather too inclined to air their opinions outside the ring, even if they have been gleaned from others with more experience.

I well remember being allotted a learner judge to whom I gave my candid opinion on the various animals that came before us. It was most unfortunate for me that my protégé was bosom friends with one lady owner, of whose animal I had not been particularly polite. When I emerged from the refreshment tent, after a cup of tea, I was tackled by the owner in question, who told me in far straighter language what she thought of me as a judge than I had told my learner what I had thought of her horse. I quickly dived back into the tent for something stronger.

A few months ago, one society held a judges' learners day. A talk was given on what to look for, then a demonstration by two well-known show riders on two well-known animals. The class was then split up into groups with other animals, their opinions were criticised and the day finished with a discussion. To those of the committee who were present, it was only too obvious how badly some of them rode and how ignorant they were on conformation and action. At the present time, some of the young tend to ride too far in front of their horses. With hollow backs, their knees far back on the saddle flaps and the reins dangling from their finger-tips, they would have little chance of managing a strong, young horse in the show ring. It is difficult to understand why this type of seat is adopted. It is not, I am sure, being taught in the Pony Club. It is possible that it may be partly due to some of the exaggerated saddles which seem to be fashionable. They were, I am told, introduced as a forward-positioned jumping saddle, when the balance of the horse is forward, and not intended to ride in normally. It is certainly most uncomfortable to try to do so. At the present time, the types of saddles judges find adorning animals in the show ring, and in particular hack classes, is almost frightening. In these, one might find jumping saddles, pony saddles, cut back show saddles and continental dressage saddles. It should be remembered that many show animals, and in particular light-weight hunters, small hunters and hacks, have been ridden practically entirely by ladies. Therefore a male judge often finds that owing to the extra weight, longer coat tails and different aids, many animals tend to put their backs up for the first couple of minutes. Consequently, if he is wise, he will maintain contact with the animal's mouth directly he gets into the saddle, he will sit rather behind the horse and maintain impulsion to prevent a buck or a kick.

I may lay myself open to criticism, but I would say that when galloping in the ring it is difficult for a judge to get the best from a horse, especially when riding a green animal, when riding short and the bottom right out of the saddle. I remember a most knowledgeable Yorkshire dealer, who un-fortunately died a few years ago, watching a class being judged. After watch-ing the judge ride a couple of horses, jockey fashion, round the ring, he turned to me and, in his broad Yorkshire dialect, said: "Yer can't judge 'osses without yer ass int saddle." It can be seen therefore, that it is ex-tremely difficult for judges to try to perform in the cut-forward, tilted up at the back, deep-seated, types of saddles. A well-worn in, fairly straight cut hunting saddle would seem to be the answer, to which a point strap has been added. I do consider a point strap is an important addition. It comes in front of the three girth straps and is fixed to the point pocket and point of the tree. If this is used, as a front girth strap, it will tend to keep the saddle back from the shoulders. It is a mystery why so many spend so much on a show animal and take so little trouble with their tack. In many cases girl riders have miniature stirrups, to show off their tiny feet and some even cut off their leathers to their exact length. It is seldom that the young make any effort to assist the judges by helping to alter the leathers or holding the stirrup.

Meditations on Judging

In nearly every class there will be a curb chain fitted over the bridoon instead of underneath.

It must surely be good policy to provide normal saddles, leathers and stirrups, supple reins, not stiff double handfuls or bootlaces, in order to try to give judges the most comfortable rides. Also, to assist them as much as possible to save time, so that they can ride as many animals as time allows.

Everybody who has spent their lives with horses, bought, sold and frequently lost money on them, have their own particular likes and dislikes on certain points of conformation and soundness. Some people, for example, can forgive curbs on the grounds that, in their experience, if fired, they seldom cause trouble. Others who have been unlucky enough to find that firing has not been really satisfactory in curing this weakness are too shy to risk buying such an animal again. There are other unsoundnesses as well, which some people, through experience, will buy at a reduced price. Consequently, although any form of unsoundness is unforgivable in the show ring, and although the majority of judges will have few differences on the main points at issue, there will be differences on the less obvious and more controversial points of conformation.

All judges, for example, will be able to recognise a good foreleg, with big enough bone to carry the weight. Some, however, will tend to overlook one very slightly back of the knee which others will not forgive. I am inclined to favour one over at the knee; so much so that I feel inclined to give it preference over one with straight conformation. If asked, I suppose my reason would be the same as I buy a certain brand of tyres—from my experience they do not wear out so quickly. On the subject of tyres, in the war many people made the mistake of buying an attractive second-hand motor car with worn tyres, only to find that new ones were unobtainable. Similarly, it is a common mistake for beginners to concentrate too much on the tops and not enough on the limbs. Also, even if they are aware of some weakness in conformation, they are inclined to overlook that weakness, because they are particularly attracted by the general impression and colour of the animal.

It is certain that nobody can be a good judge of horses without a great deal of experience and constant practice. The best possible experience is to buy, sell and lose money on the bad buys. It is also certain that no one can lay off all connection with horses for a number of months and then trust himself to sum up a class quickly and with full confidence in one's own ability.

Between the wars, most young cavalry officers and many others as well, would buy prospective hunters, point-to-pointers or polo ponies with the

Meditations on Judging

intention of enjoying themselves and with high hopes of eventually selling at a profit. Although there was no shortage of nerve there was a general lack of experience and knowledge. Consequently there were very few who did not put in a great deal of hard work and yet lose some of their original outlay, and, as the majority had little money to lose in such ventures, many hard lessons were learnt.

At the present time horses, and their keep, are very expensive, and there is an ever-increasing number of owner, groom riders and horses kept at livery. The majority of these owners seem quite content with their acquisitions and have no desire to hear of their strong or weak points. There are no prospective judges from this source.

It is strange that so many wishful buyers will slink off on their own to buy a horse when few would risk buying a motor car without guidance. Our old friend Mr. John Jorrocks says: "When three men enter a yard, a dealer seldom opens out. Two are plenty for business—if the buyer is pea-green, he had better get some riper friend to play first fiddle, and he must be spectator." On the other hand the prospective buyer might be nervous of the middlemen which are all too prevalent even today. Mr. John Jorrocks sums them up when he says: "These are the bouys to bother a dealers' vig. A vink from them stops a bargain, while an approvin' nod from such distinguished judges drives ingenuous youth into extempore bargains that they could otherwise bring half their acquaintance to inspect."

I remember watching an old dealer selling a dreadful animal, at a vast sum, to a wealthy, ignorant Know-all. I went up to him and told him it was just pure, rank robbery and he ought to be ashamed of himself. Without hesitation he turned on me and said: "You don't realise—I am a poor man and this is the only way I can steal money without being sent to prison." There was really nothing more to be said.

It would obviously be presumptuous of me to try to lay down anything definite on judging. I can only state my opinion, likes and dislikes with which some, more knowledgeable than myself, may not agree.

When a class of hunters enter the ring, I think the first thing one should consider is whether they are all up to the necessary weight required of that class. It appears to be fashionable, at the present time, for owners to enter their animals in classes when they are up to far more weight than is laid down.

A lightweight class requires a hunter to be capable of carrying not more than 13 stone, and yet a 15·3 hands animal, up to 12 stone 7 lbs., would look small and outclassed in most lightweight classes. The majority would be capable of carrying 14 stone, and should by rights be in the middleweight class. It would appear that many judges should be much more severe on this

Future champions

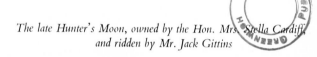

The late Hunter's Moon, owned by the Hon. Mrs. Stella Cardiff,
and ridden by Mr. Jack Gittins

Meditations on Judging

point. At the walk, I like to see a horse balanced and bridling with his head still, not crossing his jaw or reaching at the bridle. I like to see a full striding walk with the tail swinging as he goes, not short half strides, inclining to jig with the tail carried on one side. The trot should be free, balanced and smooth. There should be little or no knee action, the foreleg going well out with the maximum use of the shoulder. The toe should meet the ground first and the action so easy, balanced and light that the animal barely seems to touch the ground. I hate to see a horse punching along with his forefeet, the action coming from the knee and the heels hitting the ground first. I can see no possible object of producing an exaggerated extended trot in the show ring. This is fairly common, especially in hack classes, so much so that, when ridden by the judge, it is sometimes difficult to get the animal to trot normally. A hack should be a lovely ride in all its paces, this type of trot is jolty, uncomfortable and unnatural.

In the canter and the gallop I like to see long, low, sweeping strides. I doubt whether young judges concentrate enough on the hind leg action. I like to see the hind legs coming right forward with powerful rhythmical punches driving the horse along.

I hate to see excessive knee action, and the hind legs coming forward in short half strides, trailing further and further behind, as the pace increases.

It might appear that, by watching horses move round the ring, judges can tell the good or bad rides. This is not always the case and they get many surprises. Some horses will be mouthy, stiff, one sided, ring nappy, short in front or roll. I recall a very goodlooking horse in one class. We pulled it in top, but when ridden it felt as if it was going cross-legged behind, although it was not. When I got off I felt quite sea-sick, and after my co-judge had ridden it I asked his opinion. He took some time in answering but eventually he said: "I have got false teeth; I had such a rough ride they became misplaced and I have only just got them back again." When seeing the class stripped and in hand, I like to see an intelligent head, a wide forehead and prominent eyes. I don't like a head to be too small or too large with little room between the eyes. I like to see plenty of room between the jowl and the neck. I like to see a strong wide neck with a good length along a narrow mane and as short as possible underneath the neck. I hate a close coupled, weak, over-long necked animal as, in my experience, the majority eventually make a noise.

There is an old saying, "Quarters a necessity, shoulders a luxury", but so much depends on how a horse uses his shoulders. There can be no argument that the shoulders should slope well back, but a good shoulder is not much use if the animal is tied in at the elbow, as this will constrict movement. I like to see a strong, muscular forearm with big flat knees. I hate a foreleg tied in below or back at the knee. I like to see good flat bone below the knee with plenty of room between the cannon bone, suspensory ligament and tendons. I hate the round fleshy limbs such as the old Suffolk Punch used to suffer from. The fetlock joints should be clean and hard, not swollen, worn and puffy. The vast majority of trouble I have had has been in the feet, and I find there is not much one can do about it when once one has eliminated the ordinary minor ailments. I like well made, even, open feet, and I hate big flat or small boxy feet. The girth should be deep and big, the back short and loins strong and muscular. I always think that a horse, rather long in the back, gives one a better ride, but I try to visualise what that animal will look like after two days a week towards the end of the season. Has he the middlepiece to carry the length or will he run up too light? I don't like a horse that is slack behind the saddle or has weak loins. On the other hand I like to be able to sit into a horse and not on top of it. I like to see the tail set high on the quarters. I like to see a hind leg with length from the hip to the hock, good strong second thighs and gaskins.

The point of the hock and the back of the leg below the hock should be in a straight perpendicular line from the point of the quarters to the ground. The hocks should not be out behind the horse as, even in a young, immature animal, they seldom correct themselves. The hocks should not be too bent nor should a horse be cow or sickle hocked, but I prefer a slightly bent hock to one that is very straight. Here again, in my experience, I have found the very straight hocks are more liable to produce spavins than those that are slightly bent.

Finally, to the young and enthusiastic, who hope to become expert judges, and to the mature, whose duty it is to assist the young, I can do no better than to quote again from Mr. Jorrocks: "We must all creep afore we can walk, and all be bitten afore we can bite. But let not ingenuous youth despair. If his 'oss is not so good as he might be, let him cherish the reflection that he might have been far worse. Let him apply that moral precept so beautifully inculcated towards his better 'alf:

> Be to his faults a little blind,
> Be to his virtues ever kind."

The buyer needs a hundred eyes, the seller not one.
ITALIAN PROVERB

Mr. Sawyer Rides to Hounds

COLONEL M. P. ANSELL, C.B.E., D.S.O.

MR. SAWYER, better known to his friends as Bert, was a fine horseman, and to watch him in the hunting field was certainly an education. Barely twenty, tall and lean, like any true Englishman it was when hounds ran that all was forgotten. There are many who are great horsemen but who never learn the art of riding to hounds, and, even more, who at times forget that the true sportsman will always be thinking and planning with the hope of saving his horse so that he may be in at the end. At times it may pay to jump a large post and rails, at others it will be better to save the horse and slip through a gate. The glory of hunting is the uncertainty. When hounds run we all look forward to a hunt—perhaps, who knows, it may be the greatest of the year. In fact, just like fishing, one never knows, and so from the start of a hunt an artist such as young Bert Sawyer rides to hounds thinking and planning with the one end in view of saving his horse, Leopard, and so being in at the finish.

Leopard, a well-bred chestnut, stands about 16·2 hands, and has a few indistinct spots, hence his name. Although only six, he is well trained and full of courage, and, of course, like his master he enjoys hunting.

It was a glorious morning in January as Bert Sawyer came down the stairs. He gave the "glass" a tap—it was steady. He picked up a piece of chocolate and slipped some silver into his pocket. This latter might be useful for some friend who opens a gate, or, although he had looked at Leopard's shoes, who knows, before the day was done a shoe might be lost and a blacksmith visited. As Bert crossed the yard he picked up his saddle and double bridle, which he had cleaned and polished the night before. A good horseman is always clean and smart, and he rightly knows it is his duty to the Master to be well turned out. Leopard was quickly saddled, girths not too tight, and before he left the stable Bert bent down and picked out Leopard's feet, since his father was particular and did not like a trail left across the tidy yard.

As these two sportsmen turned out of the gate the church clock struck half-past eight; two and a half hours to ride the twelve miles, five miles per hour, and no short cuts by coverts which the Master might wish to draw later that day.

For the first mile Bert kept Leopard at a walk. He hummed and whistled. All things were certainly beautiful. A goods train pulled into the siding, and the smoke billowed slowly across the adjoining field. Certainly they were in for a good day, the barometer steady, but slightly on the rise, and now this smoke. But scent, like hunting, is uncertain.

Bert felt he must now jog on, but before doing so tightened up his girths, and, with a pat to Leopard, was away at a steady trot. He was soon joined by Farmer Welbourn and his daughter. Not only did Bert enjoy their company, but Leopard did also, for horses go better with others. Cars and horse boxes passed. What fools, Bert agreed; these people in cars did not know what they were missing. He enjoyed looking over the fences as he could see the countryside, and even Leopard laughed to himself as he thought, "I am much fitter from this road work, and my legs are hard." As they approached Aldby they were joined by more and more cars until it became quite difficult to get along the road.

Aldby, a small village with a green, was a good meet, and already Will, the Huntsman, was sitting with his hounds at the top end of the green. Bert saw Mr. Sponge, the Master, and quickly moved over to bid him, "Good morning", taking off his hat. He then walked over to Will and wished him, "Good morning", but did not worry Ernest, the Whipper-in, who was fully occupied keeping hounds up to Will for fear they might get kicked. The church clock showed ten to eleven, so he then hopped off Leopard, had a look at his feet (he might have picked up a stone), his bit, and his curb— all was well and comfortable. As he looked across the green, he could see two strangers talking to Mr. Scribe, the Hunt Secretary. They were obviously paying their "cap" and not waiting for Mr. Scribe to seek them out.

A few minutes before the hour Bert mounted and, without being noticed, moved round to a place not far from Mr. Sponge, as he was determined to move off close behind him, to make sure he was well placed from the start. As the clock struck the hour, Mr. Sponge gave a nod to Will, and they were off. Mr. Sponge is a punctual man and there is no mercy for those arriving

Mr. Sawyer Rides to Hounds

late. As we all knew, the first draw was to be Buttercrambe Thorns, a certain find, and Bert was going to make sure he was well placed. Down a side road, and across three fields, Bert kept close behind Mr. Sponge. He avoided talk, as this was no time to forget that a good start might make all the difference.

On arrival at the small thick covert, Will sent Ernest to the far end, and Mr. Sponge went to a gate in the corner and, placing his horse squarely across it, sat trying to listen. This was not easy as he was soon engulfed in a throng, many of whom seemed more interested in the gossip of the neighbouring Hunt Ball last night. Chatter, chatter, and then that ominous crack as some horse let out a kick. The offender was obviously one who believed a red ribbon in his horse's tail exonerated him from all blame. Although he wore a red coat, his voluminous hunting tie proved him without doubt no "fox-catcher".

Bert Sawyer liked to listen and plan. He did not wish to be either kicked or deafened by gossip. About thirty yards from the gate was a small post and rails. Leopard was well trained, a good timber jumper, and would not swerve, even if horses were galloping alongside. Here was the place for Bert, and so he and Leopard sat listening and waiting. Suddenly Leopard pricked his ears and at that moment came a whimper, another, and then a roar of music such as is never equalled. Will was cheering his hounds, and as Ernest holloaed there was a surge towards Mr. Sponge. He, however, stood his ground and seemed quite unmoved.

Bert turned Leopard and got square to the rails, carefully watching the Master out of the corner of his eye, as he must not jump that fence until the Master was through the gate. Mr. Sponge bent down and seemed a long time fumbling, but Bert knew he was in no hurry, for he was determined that hounds should have plenty of time in the first field—so very important to allow them to settle on the line and get away. Will blew a "gone away" on his horn and the gate was opened.

Bert collected Leopard, pushed him quickly into a canter, and over the rails into a nice field of grass, and as soon as he landed he looked at the distant fence at the far end. The field were galloping behind Mr. Sponge, heading for a gate. If Bert swung over to them he would be enmeshed in the mob. To his left front he saw another post and rails, under a large oak. Obviously the drip from the tree had killed the fence—this was his spot. He pushed Leopard along, keeping almost level with the Master, and as he approached the fence he steadied his horse into a quiet canter, ducked his head to avoid a low branch, and was over.

It certainly was a beautiful morning. As he landed he whistled and cheered to Leopard. Hounds were disappearing through the next fence, slightly to his right, and so he was down wind. This was the place to be, for if hounds turned it was likely they would turn towards him. If, however, they turned up wind, he would always hear them. The field was a wide grass one with ridge and furrow, going the way they were galloping, and so Bert swung on to the top of the ridge, where the going was good, stood up in his stirrups, and looked ahead.

The next fence, a cut and laid, looked small, but maybe there was a ditch on the far side. Will seemed to jump it perfectly and Bert could see him disappearing straight ahead. Leopard was galloping comfortably along with his head low, looking where he was going, and Bert could see Mr. Sponge out of the corner of his eye, just slightly ahead. As he approached the fence he steadied, and was over. At the same time there was a shout from that "know-all" Walter Burns, "'Ware wheat". Bert knew he had jumped into wheat and quietly pulled to the hedgerow. Here there were two alternatives. He could follow the hedge, or go out of his way by jumping out of the field into a grass one running parallel. This he and Leopard did, and then sharp right, and in front a stone wall. This looked big and he was tempted to swing to a gap, but knowing it would probably mean boulders strewn into the field on which to land, he swung to the left and jumped the high part. As he approached he pushed Leopard on, as he wanted to land well out. Farmers have a habit of leaving old ploughs, or even harrows, under a wall, and he was taking no chances.

Well over and into an old stubble field. Hounds had checked now, and Bert wondered whether the heaps of manure had anything to do with it. Anyway, he knew Will would prefer Farmer Stubbin's good farmyard manure rather than artificials. Bert Sawyer was no fool. He knew that the minute hounds checked he must stand still and not risk a rating from Mr. Sponge. The strangers walked quietly after Will and the hounds, but not for long before they heard Mr. Sponge's voice in wrath. Bert stood quite still, turned Leopard up wind so that he got plenty of air, and watched. Will was casting on to the fence in the distance. He saw three hounds feather along the fence, and they were away.

There was no great hurry, and in the next fence there was a gate. As he approached he could see the hinge was on the left, and so he moved his whip into his left hand. He held the gate and did not let it slam till young Evans came up.

Hounds were running again with a good cry across this grass field, and as they looked ahead they could see what appeared to be a thick fence. Will was over followed by Ernest, who seemed to be taking things easy, perhaps too easy, for on landing he disappeared. There must be a ditch on the far side, thought Bert, and as he approached he pushed Leopard on and landed well into the next field, a really deep and heavy plough. This would

Mr. Sawyer Rides to Hounds

take it out of Leopard, but Bert—always thinking of his horse, swung to one side where there was a furrow with standing water—to hold water there must be a hard bottom. Ahead he could see an old gate. He made for this and what a relief! No one likes jumping out of heavy plough. The gate was a broken down one, tied up with rope. Poor Will, in a great hurry, was struggling to get it undone. As Bert approached he gave a shout to Will and slipped off Leopard. He soon had the gate undone, and Will was through, followed by Mr. Sponge. Billie Smith followed Mr. Sponge through and both waited while Bert remounted.

They were now in a grass field, but hounds were disappearing through a hairy old bullfinch the far side. Bert knew he would have to push on at this, or he would stick in the middle. He chose what appeared to be a weak spot, increased his pace, and as Leopard took off, put up his right arm to save his face. He was through and into another grass field, with ridge and furrow; but this time the ridge was running across the field. Nothing tires a horse more quickly than ridge and furrow, but it has its uses if one wants to school a young horse, or muscle up a hunter. Bert turned Leopard quietly to the headland, where he could gallop in comfort.

This really was a hunt and hounds were now running well. As Bert looked ahead, he wondered. The fence looked weak, with gaps, yet in the next field bullocks were standing watching. There was probably wire on the far side, and sure enough, the next moment there was a shout from Will, "'Ware wire."

There was no gate, and as Bert reached Will he asked him to cut it. Bert slid off Leopard and Will handed him a pair of wire cutters. Will held Leopard while Bert climbed over the fence to cut the wire. This he did close to a post, so that it would be easy to mend, and so that he could avoid the loose end as it flew back. Will walked through the fence, and Bert came back to remount Leopard. Mr. Sponge had arrived and led the way through the gap, closely followed by Bert, but not too close in case the Master's horse, Bones, should have a fall. There was no hurry for hounds had checked in the field, foiled by the bullocks. Bert stood facing up wind and watched. Will rode quietly behind the feathering pack towards the next field. The field walked after Mr. Sponge, who was making for a haystack, and it was almost certain there would be a gate nearby.

As they listened they heard hounds speak again. They were certainly well away, through another gate and into a large grass field. As Bert looked towards the next fence he realised that here was a cut and laid, with what looked to be a blind ditch on the take-off side. The most unpleasant of fences, and the more so as the take-off looked poached by cattle. There was only one way to ride at a fence like this, and that was at a trot, making sure Leopard stood well back. He pulled Leopard back to a trot, and then pushed him on at what looked to be a weak spot. He was over dragging his hind legs behind him. Billie Smith had not been so lucky for he was down, and his nice grey was galloping on. Billie gave Bert a wave and he caught the grey, slipped its reins over the gate post, and galloped down a muddy lane.

Bert galloped along the middle, keeping on the hard. With a cheery shout he passed Mr. Hill, hanging on to a strong colt, on through a gate to the road, and as he passed young Lewis Hill holding the gate he threw him a sixpence, with a "Thank you."

Hounds had turned up wind. Off the road, across a field, and ahead was a wooden bridge with a gate at each end. These are often slippery. Will opened the first gate, passed it to Bert, and waited at the second before galloping on, so allowing Bert to get over the bridge. Behind Bert was young Lucy Glitters, her veil all torn but nevertheless just as attractive as she had been the night before at the Hunt Ball, or so thought Bert.

Was there anything at this moment that could compare with hunting? The country looked clear and the fields were wet, but the going was good; and here was Bert happy, with Leopard, at the head of the hunt, and what a hunt! Up wind in these waterlogged meadows hounds were racing, and their cry was thrilling. Across two fields, and Bert knew the brook, which was a formidable one, lay ahead, but Leopard was good at water. As he approached, Bert could see hounds away on the right, trying to fly the brook, and so he knew it was jumpable. The main thing was to choose a place with a good sound take-off. As Bert looked ahead he saw a clump of willows. He would keep clear of these, for they usually overhung a deep pool, where fishermen would find a nice trout under a hollow bank—friends to fishermen, but not to would-be brook jumpers. On the left some thorns; this was the place, for thorns like dry ground.

Within fifty yards Bert steadied Leopard. No great speed was required to jump water. Bert must make sure Leopard was well balanced and took off as close to the edge of the bank as possible. The last ten strides he pushed on. What a joy! He was over. Will was on the right, and there were now five of them. Poor young Gubbins was on the bank, but his horse had got out the wrong side. Lucy Glitters, in her new habit, had been in and out—but no time for this—ahead was what looked like a lane.

As so often after having crossed a brook, hounds were not running so fast. A fox seems to lose some of his scent after being in a brook. Bert chose his place with care, an old thorny fence into a lane, but what was of more importance to him was the second fence. He selected a spot opposite some rails on the far side of the lane. Quietly in and out over the rails—too easy—but, oh dear, hounds had checked.

Mr. Sawyer Rides to Hounds

Rarely did Bert jump into a field in which hounds were checked, and he moved quickly under the fence and stood quite still. It was obvious that the fox had been headed, for at the far end of the field two men were cutting the fence. They were shouting and waving towards the main road. Will was not best pleased when he saw a cur dog returning to the hedge-cutters, and he must have coursed the fox. How often does a hunt come to an end just when one had survived some obstacle such as a brook. Now he could hear the "faint-hearted" field clattering down the main road.

Will had no alternative but to lift hounds, and jumped on to the road. To avoid the many riders on the road he jumped out again at an angle. Bert rode quietly over towards the road and seeing a gate in the next field, jumped over the fence. This was nearly his undoing, for on the landing side there was a large blind ditch. Bert, fine horseman that he was, saw it in time, and as Leopard pecked he sat quite still and gave him his head. Leopard used his head and neck to regain his balance.

Will was casting parallel to the road, where hounds again picked up the line. Most of the field turned in at the first gate, but Bert could see at the far end that there were sheep penned in kale. Obviously this meant wire netting. Anyway, he was not going to get mixed up with sheep, particularly in January.

Bert could easily hear hounds who were now hunting slowly, close on the tired fox, which was twisting and turning. To Will, like every huntsman, this phase of the hunt was critical. He hoped to be able to leave hounds alone and not to be bothered by riders too close. Bert knew he might be able to help Will, particularly if he could view the fox.

He turned off the road, through a gate. The country was rough, and at the end of the field he walked through a thin old fence on a bank, across two fields, jumping the fences in gaps closed with rails. He could still hear hounds hunting slowly on his right, as he came to a big dyke. He rode Leopard down the bank, hopped over the bottom, and crawled up the far side.

Looking ahead, Bert saw what he thought was a fox. Yes, he was sure as he saw it turn through the fence, and it was the hunted one, very dirty, with his brush hanging low.

Hounds were still hunting, and Bert knew Will would not want him to holloa as this would make hounds raise their heads, and with scent failing on a tired fox, they might not gain it again.

Bert cantered quickly up to the place where he last saw Mr. Fox, stood in his stirrups, pointing Leopard's head in the direction the fox had gone. He then raised his hat. Will saw him, but as Bert expected, left his hounds alone. They hunted quietly up to Bert and through the fence. Will followed and as he passed he thanked Bert for keeping quiet.

Mr. Sawyer Rides to Hounds

Bert followed slowly after Will, who was quietly encouraging his hounds. As they approached a thick boundary fence Bert saw Will jump off, leaving his horse, and almost at once heard, "Who-whoop 'ere! Yeu wind him in there!" and "Gone to ground" blown on his horn. Bert slipped off Leopard and caught hold of Will's horse. He led both horses well away, for fear either might tread on a hound, loosened the girths, had a look round, and stood patting and thanking Leopard for the way he had carried him.

Mr. Sponge was soon on the scene, quickly followed by Billie Smith, Lucy Glitters and young Gubbins. Chatter there was in plenty; how well Snowie had jumped the brook; how annoying that young Percy Brown had been left at the start, but he had to have a word with his future mother-in-law, Mrs. Partridge. Mr. Sponge decided that it was quite hopeless to try to dig the fox out, and anyway he was a good one and had earned a reprieve. Hounds would now draw Malton Gorse.

Bert had made up his mind, and he was well satisfied. Leopard had given him a great ride, and as it was fifteen miles home, he would be on his way. He waited for Will, thanked him, and walked over to Mr. Sponge, bidding him a, "Good night and thank you, Master." He did not hang about.

As soon as he was on the road he pulled his girths up and jogged on. A drink for Leopard on the way, and he would keep jogging on, but would walk up and down steep hills, leading Leopard.

As he jogged Bert sang, and quietly thought what a lucky chap he was to have such a horse, and even more so, to have had such a good hunt. Was there anything to compare with hunting? Certainly not.

We, who had watched Bert Sawyer throughout the hunt, realised how much we could learn from him. He thought ahead and rode each varying fence correctly. He saved Leopard in the ridge and furrow, or in the plough. He jumped no unnecessary fences as he always remembered he must be there at the finish. Bert was well mannered and always ready to help. He certainly was a great horseman, but more, he knew HOW TO RIDE TO HOUNDS.

FORRARD ON
"Who is that under his horse in the brook?"
"Only Dick Christian," answers Lord Forester, "and it's nothing new to him."
"But he'll be drowned," exclaims Lord Kinnaird.
"I shouldn't wonder," observed Mr. William Coke, "but the pace is too good to inquire."

CHARLES JAMES APPERLEY (*Nimrod*)
THE CHASE

Paperchase

PHYLLIS HINTON

MY APPROACH to the job of editing an equestrian magazine has always been slightly unethical, as for a long while I prided myself on being a horsewoman first and a journalist second. For this reason I wonder whether I am fully qualified to write on this somewhat searching subject, as I feel that the model editor should be majestically detached and thus able to put before his readers a well-spiced pie which they will avidly devour even if it lacks any real food value. No, during my many years devoted to this game I have preferred to set my sights on a different target and provide what I feel they will enjoy and which may even help them on their pilgrim's progress towards the promised land of perfect horsemanship.

Should an editor be all things to all men—including, of course, women and children? That depends entirely on his readers, not on himself. To one he will always appear as a two-faced monster, to another a discerning friend; and until they tell him, he'll never realise his dual personality. Let us consider some of the people who are the bane and pleasure of an editor's life.

First of all is the Girl with the Fixation. She is a thoroughly mixed-up type, and we've all met her in some form or another. Usually she has her eyes fixed on the stars above, and because she loves and aspires to them she thinks they must be reflected in all she does. Perhaps her own joy and absorption in writing, or drawing, or schooling horses, or beatle-watching— it doesn't matter what—should be sufficient to keep her happy. But it isn't, you know. The fact that the editor fears that his readers might fail to appreciate her efforts turns her sad, sour and bitter. She is convinced that it is all a ramp, that the budding genius hasn't a chance to ripen, or to get a foot round the door, because the privileged few who have somehow bought their way to fame have helped to bar it against her. She becomes a positive menace and haunts the dreams of any editor foolish enough to take her seriously.

Next is the Adventurer. Usually he is very clever, if perhaps a trifle

Paperchase

unbalanced, both emotionally and in his business relationships. He steps right out of the pages of the Arabian Nights—an adventurer in the most delightful sense of the word, and a convicing one at that, colourful and flaunting a Continental title.

Perhaps he wants to write for your magazine, or to represent it abroad—this latter because it may give him an entrée he could not otherwise obtain. Filled with charm, he will probably arrive at the Editorial offices with masses of spring flowers—perhaps, like himself, just past their best—will wander on across the world, eventually meeting a lady of his own age who will marry and maintain him as the real life manifestation of the dreams which so seldom come true. The marriage may be a success if she is wise enough to continue to kid herself and not to expect from him more than good looks and good manners.

As one titled polo player from a mountainous mid-European country once pointed out to me, "The only unforgivable sin is that of bad manners." He seemed to have experimented in a big way before coming to this conclusion. The soundest advice I can give other editors who meet would-be contributors such as these is: lock up your secretaries—for their own good, of course!

In addition to the problems there are many compensations in the life of any editor, particularly of one who is dedicated to horses. There is the some-what fearful thrill of seeing advance copies of your magazine arrive from the printers and thinking "Ah! The beautiful horse (or whatever it may be) on the cover really is an inspiration—worth looking at again and again. There is something in this issue for every member of a horsey family to enjoy or profit by. How nice this or that illustrated article looks. And thank heaven those last-minute corrections were carried out."

Speaking of corrected proofs, how grim is the occasion when the printers, usually the most co-operative and hard-working chaps, have made the requisite alteration but in doing so have dropped out or misplaced a whole line of type, or made some other mistake, possibly a spelling error, which cannot now be rectified. This is indeed shame-making, as in the eyes of the readers the unfortunate editor is guilty of unforgivable carelessness, which they much enjoy pointing out to him. How little they know of the techni-calities of how a paper or magazine is first "made up" and then "put to bed" and of the time factor, which can sometimes play such havoc with the editorial nerves.

The correspondent who is late with his "copy", the important fixture which should be written up in the next issue but which clashes with the press date, the number of advertising pages which, at the very last minute, may affect the amount of space allocated to the editorial—all these hazards and many others cause him to feel like the illustration on the cover of the old-fashioned children's book, *Struwwel Peter*—in desperate straits, with every hair on end. It is surprising that there is not a greater incidence of ulcers, heart attacks and over-doses of sleeping pills among those who minister to the apparently overwhelming literary and artistic requirements of the equestrian public.

Jealousy rears its ugly head, too. Include—unwittingly—one letter from a breeder who is seriously at odds with another and you may find yourself in need of an armed guard. Or publish an article which: (a) gives well-deserved publicity to certain horses or ponies and riders but not to others—there is not room to mention them all and how boring it would be if one did; or (b) infer that such and such an animal is not a world beater; or (c) fail to give sufficient space to some facet of the horse world of interest only to the minority of one's readers. Do any of these things and you will learn that you are susceptible to bribes, stupid, short-sighted and without integrity.

Beware of the journalist with a chip on his shoulder, of the writer who criticises what he has not actually seen for himself or knows nothing about. So many people who may have attended the *Horse and Hound* ball, or Badminton, or thrown a leg over a horse at some time in their lives, think they know everything there is to know not only on equestrian subjects but on what the public wants to read. Knowledgeable horsemen, such as, perhaps, Colonel Podhajsky, Director of the Spanish Riding School, are modest, not dogmatic, in their statements and point out that they will never cease to learn. The fact that "empty vessels make the most noise" applies particularly to some exponents of equestrian subjects.

A professional journalist, trained by experience, will usually provide a far more interesting and polished article than a star rider, unless the latter is particularly gifted. "Rapier" (Vincent Orchard), for example, would give one a better, more complete and thrilling picture of a day at Sandown Park than, say, one of our leading jockeys—unless much of his material was re-written for him. The good journalist who loves and understands his subject will know how to prepare his canvas and create a picture with a proper background, alive with colour and contrast as well as human and equine interest. He will have learned the value and meaning of words, and by using them sparingly and correctly he will have no difficulty in causing a picture to flash instantly before his readers' eyes. Even the greatest jockey would be unlikely to write with the sparkle, the wit and the observation of "Rapier", who has studied many hundreds of racehorses as well as races, even if he has not ridden in them, and journalists of his calibre often have a very practical knowledge of their subject. They are sufficiently detached to take a wide view of it—more so, sometimes, than the individual who is directly involved.

Paperchase

It is equally true that the press itself can be the editor's worst enemy because it can provide his directors with the wrong impression of what his public really wants. Take hunting. This is a subject which is very popular with readers of horsey magazines. Yet some of the daily papers give the impression that it is on the way out—is kept going by the Die-Hard brigade.

I think the following story will give some idea of the difficulties and general hazards in the life of a good hunting correspondent who, for obvious reasons, is indeed an asset to any magazine which portrays British field sports. A friend of mine set sail for Ireland with a view to covering several packs. On one of these occasions he arrived, as arranged, in an Irish dealer's yard and the dealer produced both a generous stirrup cup and an excellent type of hunter whose make and shape was not easy to fault.

Fortified by the wine of the country and the sight of a good horse the unsuspecting hunting correspondent mounted and set off in the direction of the meet. He had several minor adventures on the way as the horse did not like the passing cars and shied at anything it saw coming out of either a hedge or a gate. On arrival at the meet it became very restive and was evidently rarin' to go.

A fox was found at the first draw and hounds went away on a screaming scent. The first obstacle our correspondent encountered was a stiff post and rails which the horse did not like the look of, but his rider knew the game and sat down and drove him on. The animal hit the top rail and fell on the landing side. My friend remounted and met a second post and rails, which they cleared in splendid style. However, it was a different story when a "hairy" bank appeared on the horizon. He quickly appreciated the situation, deciding that an Irish farmer mounted on a good cob would be the ideal pilot to follow at a safe distance over this obstacle.

The horse jumped on to the bank but made an error in changing legs to jump off and our correspondent was once again on the ground. When remounted the horse showed excellent form over the numerous banks and odd pieces of timber that followed.

On returning to the dealer's yard at the end of the day my friend enquired how many times the horse had been hunted. The reply was, "Och, this is the first time the hoss has been out hunting and sure he's done mighty well if he's only fallen twice." The safe return of both horse and rider was celebrated in Irish whiskey, which probably tasted of the good water which is found in an Irish bog, although considerably more fiery. The next day this intrepid correspondent had a bit of a headache, but he was never able to decide whether this was caused by his adventures in the hunting field or his celebrations when he returned home.

Harvey Smith riding the Canadian horse, O'Malley, a big winner in this country for the past two seasons

Paperchase

I agree with Jorrocks that one can say what one likes about a person's morals but not about his horsemanship, and the press needs to be very tactful when reporting horse shows. On one occasion the correspondent of a famous periodical was at a loss to describe how a certain animal was rather a bad mover. In his account he pointed out what a wonderful horse he was standing still. This did not exactly please the owner, but it was the truth and neither the judges nor the exhibitor could take exception to it.

There is also the true story of the contributor who went on to a show ground having just returned from the Dublin Horse Show, where, at the request of a Sunday paper, he had sent them a 250-word résumé of this great Irish show. He was suddenly confronted by a doughty matron who told him in no mean way that she was the special correspondent of this particular paper and that he must lay off it in future.

The same well-known correspondent was having a drink in the bar at a famous horse show, when up sprang another lady dragon of the show-ring and made the somewhat astonishing statement that no show correspondent dare cross her. I mention these two particular instances to illustrate that it is essential for an equestrian correspondent to have a sense of humour to fit any occasion.

What is the right definition of the word "honest"? The dictionary tells us that it means "full of honour: just: the opposite to thievish, free from fraud: frank, fair-seeming, openly shown: chaste". Some horse-lovers have a strongly personal interpretation of honesty, and it is not always easy for an unfortunate editor to see a clear way through some of the very tricky situations which can arise because of this. I have known more than one individual of great character so dedicated to their particular objective for the betterment of the horse—his breed or his performance—that they have resorted to methods which, on the face of it, were wrong even if they achieved apparently good results. Yet these people were convinced that they were right and therefore above criticism. They were completely true to their own ideals and, in their own opinion, completely honest. Nothing ever changed this conviction and never could they understand why anyone should think badly of them.

Perhaps it is this way of looking at things, this unique devotion to a cause or a breed, which gives so much spice and melodrama to the horse world, besides preparing such a variety of traps for an editor or correspondent. This leads me to yet another amusement or sport inextricably tied up with horses—romance. Love affairs are so violent if they are connected with the hunting field or the show ring—or even with pony trekking. It must be that the shining horses—sons and daughters of the morning—provide just

Colonel Dan Corry, a member of the famous Irish Free State jumping team of the 'thirties, in action at the Dublin Horse Show

that touch of primeval thrill which adds such zest to the age-old game. It is true, too, that in the equestrian world two people have only to be seen having lunch or tea together to provide plenty of amusing chat for the School for Scandal. Sometimes it seems as if it is not even necessary for them to be of the opposite sex. Oh, well . . . !

Well did that great man, I think it was Sir Walter Scott, but if it warn't 'twas little Bartley, the bootmaker, say, that there was no young man wot would not rather have a himputation on his morality than on his 'ossmanship.

R. S. SURTEES, 1803–1864

*I will not change my horse with any that treads but on four pasterns . . . .
When I bestride him, I soar, I am a hawk ; he trots the air ; the earth sings when he touches it ; the basest horn of his hoof is more musical than the pipe of Hermes.*

SHAKESPEARE

The difference between a natural and an artificial seat is that in the former case the rider adapts himself to his horse, whereas in the latter the horse is adapted to the rider. Of the two the former is the easier to acquire.

CAPRILLI

THE OLDEST HORSE

According to the best authenticated records the title goes to Old Billy, a draught horse that died in England in 1822 at the almost incredible age of 63 years. He was pensioned off three years before his death, towing a boat on the River Mersey.

The chief evidence of a rider's incompetence is his horse: it is lucky the witness cannot speak.

ALVISI

Page 216. Sitting pretty at Melbourne, Australi
Page 217. Disputing the lead at Plumpton

With the Puckeridge foxhounds between Westmill and Buntingford

A huntsman grey, who blew them away, with the note of a true hound-lover

A Winter's Tale

THE HON. JOHN LAWRENCE

FROM AGINCOURT to D-Day, France, I suppose, has been the scene of more brave deeds by Englishmen than any other country in the world. Mostly, of course, they were inspired by the horrid waste of war, but sport in its less serious tragic way can also lift a man to heights of daring and achievement, and as Fred Winter and Mandarin came back last Sunday after winning the Grand Steeplechase de Paris [1962], I like to think that the ghosts of long-dead English horsemen rode beside them, glad and proud to know that the flag for which they fought and died still flies, even in this sad, dull and mechanical age.

To win at all would have been a famous victory—to win as Winter and Mandarin did was an heroic triumph over odds so steep that no normal man or horse could have been blamed for giving up long before the end.

None of this, of course, could even be guessed at, as, in the atmosphere of a Turkish bath, the fourteen runners swept gaily past the stands for the first of three intricate, twisting circuits.

So far as one could see in the friendly but chaotic tangle that serves Auteuil for a parade ring, the French horses were not a wildly impressive sight. Nor, to someone who had never seen him before, would Mandarin have been, but to the large band of English supporters the sheen on his coat, the hard muscles writhing over his quarters, and the way he pulled "Mush" Foster round the paddock all told their own encouraging tale.

Sure enough, after flicking neat and fast over the preliminary hurdle jumped on the way to the start, Mandarin was soon upsides in front and

" . . . and as Mandarin came back, a cheer went up such as
I have never heard on any racecourse"

passed the stands pulling, as usual, like a train. He has always been a "heavy-headed" ride with precious little feeling in his mouth—and always runs in a rubber-covered snaffle to save his lips and jaws.

At the beginning of last season a brand-new bridle was bought—and Mandarin had worn it only half a dozen times, including both his victories in the Hennessey and Cheltenham Gold Cups. But the trouble with rubber bits is that a fault or wear can develop unseen in the steel chain—and this, no doubt, is what had happened now.

After the first, sharp, left-hand bend the Grand Steeple course comes back towards the stands, and there, going to the fourth, a soft but staring privet fence the best part of six feet high, the bit snapped clean in the middle, inside Mandarin's mouth. I remember thinking at the time "he got a little close to that one", but for another full circuit none of us in the stands realised the dreadful truth.

In fact, of course, Fred Winter now had no contact whatsoever with the horse's mouth or head. The reins, kept together by the Irish martingale (or "rings") were still round Mandarin's neck—and they, together with the thin neck-strap of the breast-girth, were Winter's only hand hold.

To visualise the full impossibility of the situation you must remember first that when a racehorse, particularly a hard-pulling 'chaser, is galloping on the bit, much of the jockey's weight is normally balanced, through the reins, against that of the horse's head and forehand. Now, for both Fred Winter and Mandarin, this vital counterbalance was gone completely. The man, with no means of steering but his weight, had to rely entirely on grip and balance—the horse, used to steady pressure on his mouth, had to jump twenty-one strange and formidable obstacles with his head completely free —a natural state admittedly, but one to which Mandarin is wholly unaccustomed.

Small wonder then that at the huge "Rivière de la Tribune"—the water in front of the stands—he fiddled awkwardly, landing only inches clear of the bank and disaster. Thereafter, save for another nasty moment at the same fence next time round, the little horse jumped unbelievably well—Fred Winter, sitting still or driving on as the need arose, matched his every move with the sympathetic rhythm that is nine-tenths of horsemanship.

But the fences, needless to say, were only half the problem. Walking the course that morning with Winter, Dave Dick and Joe Lammin, Fulke Walwyn's head lad, we had all wondered afresh at the many turns and countless opportunities for losing your way. The Grand Steeple is, roughly, two figures of eight in opposite directions and one whole circuit outside both. There are at least four bends through 180 degrees, and to negotiate them all

Fred Winter and Mandarin: they share a place among the immortal names of sport

as Winter and Mandarin did, without bit or bridle, was, quite literally, miraculous.

The answer lies, of course, in many things—in the matchless strength of Winter's legs, in Mandarin's own good sense—and in the absolute determination of them both never to give up while there was one shot, however forlorn, left on the board.

It is also, I think, only fair to give some credit—and our thanks—to the French jockeys, several of whom could, had they pleased, have taken advantage of the disaster and, without much risk to themselves, got rid of the bigger danger. Instead, at least one—Laumas on Taillefer—and probably several others, actually did their best to help, proving gloriously that the comradeship of dangers shared can, in *some* sports at least, count far more than international rivalry.

Throughout the race, save for a moment on the last bend, Mandarin was up in the first four—and, as he jumped the Rivière for the last time, the full horror of his situation dawned upon us in the stands.

From that moment on, the nerve-racking suspense, the wild impossible hope, plunging to black despair and back again, were like nothing I have ever known on a racecourse—or for that matter anywhere else.

Mandarin cleared with ease the tricky post and rails at which he hesitated fatally three years ago—and came to the junction of the courses close fourth—close enough to lift the hearts of those who knew his and Winter's invincible finishing power.

But now disaster almost struck. Before the last right-handed turn a large bush must be passed on the left—but can with equal ease be passed on the right. Mandarin, on the inside, with no rail to guide him, could not know until the last moment which way to go. For a few heart-stopping strides he hesitated, Winter threw all his strength and weight into one last desperate swerve—and somehow they were safe.

But priceless lengths had been lost and now, round the final bend, with only two obstacles to jump, Mandarin was only fifth, some six or seven lengths behind the leader.

On the turn, of course, Winter could hardly ride at all, but then, facing the Bullfinch, in a straight line for home at last it was a different matter. From the stands we saw the familiar crouching drive of the shoulders, and Mandarin, responding as he always has and always will, thrust out his gallant head and went for the Bullfinch like a tank facing tissue paper.

None will ever know what the little horse felt or thought between those last two fences. I have always believed he knows just what it means to win—and now none will ever convince me otherwise. In a hundred desperate yards he passed three horses as if they were walking, and, as he landed in front on the long run-in, my eyes, I am not ashamed to say, were half-blind with tears.

But it was not over yet. Mandarin was deadly tired, and Winter, the reins gathered useless in his left hand, could do nothing to hold him together. He could only push and drive—and how he drove. Even so, inch by inch, Lumino, the only French horse able to accelerate, crept nearer and nearer.

In the final desperate strides, not knowing the angle, not one of us could really tell who had won. Fred Winter thought he had got up, but *he* could not speak, so for several ghastly moments we had to sweat it out. But then, there it was—number one in the frame—and as Mandarin came back, mobbed as no film star has ever been, head down, dog-tired, sweating —but surely happy—a cheer went up such as I have never heard on any racecourse.

For Fred Winter it was not the end. Riding a dream of a race, he went on, 40 minutes later, to win the Grande Course de Haies on Beaver II. I have neither time nor space to describe that race, and, triumph though it was for Beaver's trainer, Ryan Price, it only served as the perfect ending to an historic afternoon. For on Sunday, Fred Winter and Mandarin had earned themselves a place among the immortal names of sport. I have never seen a comparable feat, never expect to—and can only thank God that I was there.

CAVALCADE

This Cavalcade of Grace now stands, it speaks in silence. Its story is the story of this land.

Where in this wide world can man find nobility without pride, friendship without envy or beauty without vanity? Here, where grace is laced with muscle, and strength by gentleness confined.

He serves without servility; he has fought without enmity. There is nothing so powerful, nothing less violent; there is nothing so quick, nothing more patient.

England's past has been borne on his back. All our history in his industry: we are his heirs, he our inheritance.

Ladies and Gentlemen:

THE HORSE

RONALD DUNCAN
*Epilogue written for the
Horse of the Year Show*